DEEP
WOODS

DEEP WOODS

John Burroughs

Edited and Introduced by
Richard F. Fleck

SYRACUSE UNIVERSITY PRESS

First Syracuse University Press Edition 1998
98 99 01 02 03   6 5 4 3 2 1

All text illustrations courtesy of Jean Fader.

This book is published with the asistance of a grant
from the John Ben Snow Foundation.

Originally published in 1990 by Gibbs Smith, Publisher.

The paper used in this publication meets the minimum requirements
of American National Standard for Information Sciences—Permanence
of Paper for Printed Library Materials, ANSI Z39.48-1984. ∞™

Library of Congress Cataloging-in-Publication Data

Burroughs, John, 1837-1921.
Deep Woods / John Burroughs : edited and introduced by Richard F.
Fleck. — 1st Syracuse University Press ed.
p.   cm.
Originally published: Salt Lake City : Peregrine Smith Books,
c1990, in series: Peregrine Smith literary naturalists.
ISBN 0-8156-0416-5 (pbk.)
1. Natural history—United States.   2. Nature.   I. Fleck, Richard
F., 1937– .   II. Title.
QH81.B9233   1998
814.4—dc21   97-32702

Manufactured in the United States of America

CONTENTS

John Burroughs at the Ledges. Drawing by Jean Fader.

INTRODUCTION

From the front porch of John Burroughs's Wood-chuck Lodge near Roxbury, New York, the visitor is treated to a sweeping view of the western Catskills. These ancient mountains remain refreshingly wild even though they are but a two-hour drive from the Big Apple. Two summits (Slide and Hunter) rise above four thousand feet, and scores of peaks crest at thirty-five hundred feet and higher, high enough to be fringed with a Canadian balsam zone above densely forested slopes of maple, oak, aspen, birch, and ash. October frosts tinge these woodlands with an array of colors from purples to scarlets and yellows and leave them looking like an artist's palette.

But perhaps springtime is an even better season than autumn in the Catskill Mountains. You would think it was October with all those swollen red buds, except that thoughts of colder days and snow dissolve amid a chorus of spring pippers in the low-lying marshes. The lightness of air, the smells of earth, and the sound of ice-free waterfalls rejuvenate the spirit in ways no other season can. On just such a day I made the first of my three ascents of Slide Mountain.

During the month of May I had read John Bur-roughs's *Riverby,* containing an exciting account of his climb of Slide Mountain, at 4,203 feet, the highest in the Catskills. I had seen these mountains in the misty distance, and they always appeared as alluring as the landscapes in Washington Irving's "Rip Van Winkle." The end of the month found me dashing along the Slide Mountain trail from Big Indian Valley, the Catskills rising around me like dreamy watercolorings with the slightest tinge of green in the grey.

Myriad blossoms of white beam *(sorbus aria)* set the dense undergrowth of the maple-beech forest aglow with a silent but colorful aria. I crossed ancient riverbeds of faded maroon-colored stones and bounded upward into the ferny forest, where the dead leaves of autumn betrayed the delicate footfalls of chipmunks. Thrushes and vireos chirped in the hollow aisles of the forest.

After being somewhat spoiled by a level section of trail, I began a long and gradual ascent at an angle of about forty-five degrees, following piles of those pale maroon boulders until I reached a thirty-five-hundred-foot elevation marker. Here the trees had only begun to bud; I had returned to April. Instead of lush fern fronds, I saw only fiddleheads barely breaking through the ground. The *sorbus aria*'s veiny, heart-shaped leaves were much smaller, though rings of white blossoms had already come out. Yellow birches appeared stark and nude against the sky, as did all other species save the balsam firs.

Echoes from a woodpecker rose up from the lower vales. Some three hundred vertical feet higher, the trees began to show signs of dwarfing. A few wild cherry trees looked as gaunt as desert vegetation. Northern birds like longspurs chirped away in the treetops; perhaps they would remain here for another few weeks before their departure to arctic Canada. I caught my first glimpse of the hazy, almost milky, valleys below through the branches of the cool forest. At thirty-nine hundred feet, I entered a distinct Laurentian forest zone dominated by rich and fragrant balsam fir that reminded me of coastal trails on Monhegan Island, Maine.

At last I stood on the summit atop a rock slide, well over four thousand feet above the sea. Panther, Wittenberg, Cornell, and Peekamoose mountains spread beyond in misty space. The lead grey Shokan Reservoir appeared more like sky than water. Was it the mystical entrance to some lower world? I was reminded of what John Burroughs wrote about Slide Mountain's summit: "All was mountain and forest on every hand. Civilization seemed to have done little more than to have scratched this rough, shaggy surface of the earth here and there. In any such view, the wild, the aboriginal, the geographical greatly predominate. The works of man dwindle, and the original features of the huge globe come out."

Yes, it is a sense of the entire globe that comes to the mountaineer. Perhaps this global awareness helps account for the feeling that one is standing in the midst of some sanctum sanctorum. Burroughs felt it on Slide Mountain; Thoreau experienced it on Katahdin; and John Muir most certainly felt it in the high Sierra. In *Riverby* Burroughs muses: "It was on Mount Horeb that God appeared to Moses in the burning bush, and on Sinai that he delivered to him the law. Josephus says that the Hebrew shepherds never pasture their flocks on Sinai, believing it to be the abode of Jehovah. The solitude of mountain-tops is peculiarly impressive, and it is certainly easier to believe the Deity appeared in a burning bush there than in the valley below."

I sat back to enjoy the notes of the white-throated sparrows and Swainson's thrushes; those bird songs erased the years. *Ah tee tee tee tee* came from one perch, and from another, the whirling sound of a thrush: *a myrtle, a turtle, a whirtle, a myrtle.* Was I still a boy in the Maine woods? No wonder Rip Van Winkle lost twenty years here in the Catskills!

A faint rumbling came from cloudy western skies, but I wanted to experience the slide side of Slide Mountain before my descent. I did the reverse of John Burroughs, who writes: "It was ledge upon ledge, precipice upon precipice, up which and over which I made my way slowly and with great labor, now pulling myself up by my hands, then cautiously finding niches for my feet and zigzagging right and left from shelf to shelf."

Along the rocky trail I noticed "pudden" stone, a conglomerate usually found at the base of coal veins. And to my joy, I stumbled across a solitary yellow lily growing in between the mossy slabs of the steep eastern slope. After a half-hour's descent, I peered out into green space straight down. This side of the mountain is said to have the general configuration of a giant horse with lowered head. Burroughs speculates that if the horse ever reared its head, Slide Mountain would look down upon Mount Marcy, the highest of the Adirondacks, and even the White Mountains of New Hampshire.

From this sheer vantage point, I gingerly retraced my steps to the summit and proceded down the back side to Big Indian Valley where it started to rain. Wisps of mist slithered upslope to settle in the wind.

In this country John Burroughs (1837-1921) was born and raised. As a young farm boy near Roxbury, Burroughs, the seventh of ten children, learned to lay stone fences (as in Robert Frost's poem "Mending Wall"), tap maple trees for sugar, shear sheep, gather flax, thresh oats and rye, and pick apples. In his spare time he would go trout fishing, watch birds, or sit on the Rundle place rock, upon which Woodchuck Lodge now sits, to listen to the wind in the leaves of a sheltering ironwood tree.

He developed a passion for reading which sometimes caused him to neglect his chores. But his interest in books eventually led him to study at Cooperstown Academy, where he first became acquainted with the writings of Ralph Waldo Emerson and Samuel Johnson whom he imitated as a young writer. His keen interest in reading further stimulated his desire to become a nature writer. Knowing he could not support himself by his pen alone, he tried his hand at teaching in Catskill country schools and eventually New Jersey and Illinois. After marrying the very practical-minded Ursula North, who remained an obsessive housecleaner until her death, Burroughs began publishing natural history essays in the early 1860s in such journals as *Every Saturday* (in which Whitman's poetry appeared), *Knickerbocker Magazine, Putnam's Monthly Magazine,* and the *Atlantic Monthly.*

In 1863 Burroughs took a position with the U.S. Treasury Department in Washington, D.C., where he and Ursula remained for nine years. Fortunately Burroughs found much time to ramble in the nearby woodlands, to read writers like Emerson and Thoreau, and to continue writing natural history. He published his first collection of essays, *Wake-Robin,* in 1871 while still in Washington. He never found writing to be difficult in spite of his full-time employment with the government. He writes, "a written work consists of laying words together as a wall-builder fits boulders into his wall."

While in Washington, Burroughs met not only President Abraham Lincoln but also Walt Whitman; in fact he and Whitman became close friends and walked many a woodland path together. His fine account of the poet, *Notes on Walt Whitman as Poet and Person,* was published in 1867. He also developed literary friendships with David Wasson, a writer for the *Atlantic Monthly,* E. M. Allen, and Thoreau enthusiast Myron Benton, who introduced Burroughs to Thoreau's *Walden* and *The Maine Woods.*

After leaving Washington, D.C., Burroughs and his wife moved back to the Catskill Mountains where he would earn his keep as a writer and fruit farmer. And write he did at his Riverby residence (swept so clean by Ursula)—at least a half-dozen volumes between 1875 and 1886. Burroughs grew fonder each year of Thoreau's *Walden* for its spiritual discoveries and accurate reportage. He disliked nature fakers, as he called them, like Ernest Thompson Seton and Reverend William Long for their mawkish sentimentality and inaccurate reporting of natural fact. President Roosevelt became his strong ally in his campaign against nature faking, which he forcefully expressed in an *Atlantic Monthly* article. Truth, beauty, altruism, duty and the like, he said, are foreign to lower animals; animals should not be seen as half man. The nature essayist must attempt to induce in his reader a sense of self-revelation.

In 1899 John Burroughs was invited by E. H. Harriman, the New York railway tycoon, to join an expedition to coastal Alaska. There he would meet John Muir, George Bird Grinnell, and R. Swain Gifford, among others. In vast, gigantic Alaska Burroughs quickly sensed a "cosmic chill" he had not known back in the rather tame Catskills. Burroughs defined this sense of cosmic chill as an almost uncomfortable astonishment at a terribly awesome and sublime nature. Ten years later John Muir invited him to come see more of the awesome West in the Grand Canyon, Yosemite, and the Hawaiian Islands.

From 1908 until his death in 1921, John Burroughs summered at the Woodchuck Lodge near Roxbury where, like Mark Twain in Elmira, New York, he wrote voluminously (including *The Summit of Years, Time and Change, The Breath of Life,* and *Under the Apple Trees*).

This volume includes representative natural history essays from numerous works spanning John Burroughs's productive years from *Wake-Robin* (1871) to *Time and Change* (1912). It includes essays on the four seasons, his beloved Catskill Mountains, the Adirondacks, the Maine woods, and the far West of Yosemite and coastal Alaska.

Both "The Adirondacks" and "Birch Browsings" come from Burroughs's first nature volume, *Wake-Robin,* written while he was living in Washington, D.C. In his preface to this volume, Burroughs writes: "This is mainly a book about Birds, or more properly an invitation to the study of Ornithology, and the purpose of the author will be carried out in proportion as it awakens and stimulates the interest of the reader in this branch of Natural History." Burroughs's own interest in ornithology was sparked in 1863 by his first encounter with John James Audubon's writings, which was like the "bringing together of fire and powder!" However, as his biographer Clara Barrus mentions in *John Burroughs: Boy and Man* (1920), he eventually outgrew his habit of shooting birds à la Audubon in order to study them closely. (It had never occurred to young Burroughs and other early-day ornithologists to study birds with opera glasses.)

During a hot summer (1863), Burroughs, E. M. Allen and Myron Benton escaped the sweltering streets of Washington to camp in the Adirondacks of upstate New York for two weeks. He had hoped to spot a variety of birds but found them only in clearings and rarely in the deep woods (though two-dozen species are mentioned in this essay). Like Thoreau in the Maine woods, he mused over the plaintive notes of the white-throated sparrow.

But if he didn't see many birds in the Adirondacks, he did experience a novel wilderness of caves, mountains, lakes, and above all, towering "mammoth" pines. Along the shores of a "wild and desolate" lake, Burroughs marveled at the graceful flight of a great blue heron sailing from treetop to treetop. Such wild lakes, he believed, further enhanced one's sense of the wild, especially when one paddled on their surface in the light of the moon and stars. On one occasion, while night hunting from a canoe, he believed that he and his companions had entered a "land of shadows and of spectres," so black were the waters. One of the spectres with bright and infernal eyes, alas, turned out to be a victim of their hunting: a young doe. Such an event, however, was balanced by awesome views of Indian Pass and Mount Marcy, which intensified John Burroughs's sense of the wild and offered a necessary reprieve from his desk job in the nation's capital.

During the hot and sultry summer of 1868 in Washington, Burroughs dashed off to his beloved Catskills to cool off and experience the novelty of being lost on birchy summits and in deep vales, the subject of "Birch Browsings." He and two others had hoped to go "trouting" at Thomas's Lake by hiking over the top of a mountain where they had to "bear well to the left." Not bearing well enough to the left, they missed the way and had to camp atop the mountain that night. Burroughs determined to locate the lake by himself and signal his companions with rifle fire, but although he found the lake, he was too far away for his friends to hear the shots. Back on the mountaintop, he and his friends descended together, but this time into alder swamps. Were they under some spell? The cheery notes of a robin encouraged them onward until they at last stood on the shoreline of the elusive lake. Though Burroughs and his companions had been in the woods only forty-eight hours, he felt as though "we were some months, if not years, older ... Yet younger, too,— though this be a paradox,—for the birches had infused into us some of their own suppleness and strength."

A second volume written in Washington entitled *Winter Sunshine* came out in 1875, from which "The Snow-Walkers" has been selected. This essay is, perhaps, more philosophical and poetic than the two earlier ones. Its focus is winter animals whose tracks reveal a story of predation. The barking of a fox in the winter woods, Burroughs writes, "is refreshing to the ear, and one delights to know that such wild creatures are among us." He recalls that while hunting a fox, he became so captivated by its beauty and grace that he no longer had any desire to kill it. Sounding somewhat reminiscent of Thoreau in "Higher Laws" of *Walden*, Burroughs comes to realize that one is better off hunting the spiritual essence of an animal than its carcass and hide. Other animals of the snowy woods garner his attention as well, including the partridge, squirrel, skunk, and raccoon.

Another essay from *Winter Sunshine*, "Autumn Tides," focuses upon the coming of fall to the Catskills, the first sign being the spreading of thistledown by the winds. And yet when autumn's steady advance meets the equilibrium of an October Indian summer, its progress seems to halt in the leaf-checkered sunshine. Even witch hazel blooms in a mirror image of spring. Burroughs writes, "Spring is the inspiration, fall the expiration." How difficult it is for the artist to paint the

Woodchuck Lodge. Drawing by Jean Fader.

difference between April and November in the Catskills. However, fall is the season for the pen, when the fruits of the mind have fully ripened, stimulated by the crimson leaves of the dwarf sumac or the delicate plum color of the ash tree.

Four years later Burroughs came out with *Locusts and Wild Honey* (1879), from which "A Bed of Boughs" has been taken. Written as a first-person narrative, this essay takes the reader on a one-week camping trip in August into the heart of the Catskills around Peekamoose Mountain. We, too, sleep under the stars on a bed of boughs along with John Burroughs and his army-veteran friend. The reader may be reminded of Isaac Walton's *The Complete Angler* or Ernest Hemingway's "The Big Two-Hearted River." Like Hemingway's Nick Adams, Burroughs expresses sheer joy in hooking a trout, only to lose it after a ten-to-fifteen-minute struggle. Such intense moments in the woods are worth hours elsewhere. "A Bed of Boughs" has the effect of relaxing the reader from his daily tensions as he vicariously savors the scent of balsam, views of the mountains, nighttime campfire chat, and even the sounds of distant lumbermen mollified by a vast wind harp of trees.

During the summer of 1876, Burroughs made a trip to the wilds of Maine up the Kennebec River Valley to Moxie Lake, and eventually Bald Mountain along the shores of Moosehead Lake. His guide, Uncle Nathan, Clara Barrus mentions, was "as good a talker as John Muir." The essay, "A Taste of Maine Birch," (published in the volume *Signs and Seasons,* 1886) is reminiscent of Henry David Thoreau's accounts of three excursions to Maine described in *The Maine Woods* (1864). Both authors botanize, fish, hunt, canoe, and marvel at their guide's woodcraft. An even more striking parallel between Thoreau and Burroughs is their mystical reflection on the nature of the wilderness, particularly wild mountains. For Thoreau it was Mount Katahdin, an unfinished part of the globe which reminded him of a place where the Greek god Vulcan might still be at work. For Burroughs at Bald Mountain, "one seemed to be face to face with the gods of the fore-world."

There are other similarities: Uncle Nathan is much like Thoreau's first guide, Uncle George McCauslin, a self-sufficient woodsman; both Thoreau and Burroughs are quite taken by the almost supernatural qualities of the northern loon, and both writers precede John McPhee in their admiration of the beauty and poetic grace of the birchbark canoe. If there is too much wanton killing of birds and quadrupeds in Burroughs's woodsy account, it is balanced by the release of a large catch of trout at the close of the essay.

"Spring Jottings" (from *Riverby*, 1894) is a nice sampling of springtime journal entries spanning 1879 to 1891. As a preface to his selections, Burroughs comments on the virtues of keeping a journal: "To a countryman, especially of a meditative turn, who likes to preserve the flavor of the passing moment, or to a person of leisure anywhere, who wants to make the most of life, a journal will be found a great help. It is a sort of deposit account wherein one saves up bits and fragments of his life that would otherwise be lost to him." These bits and fragments consist of observations (springtime fog on a riverbank, the silver loop of sound made by the song sparrow), factual details (deep snow can draw frost out of the ground), and expressions of personal desire (one could almost eat the springtime turf like a horse). These jottings stir in us all memories of the opening and progress of spring.

E. H. Harriman invited Burroughs in 1899 to explore

coastal Alaska as the "historian" of the expedition
which took them through the inland waterway to Sitka,
Yakutat Bay, Kodiak Island, and points northwest all
the way to Siberia. The portion of the trip included here
is from "Green Alaska" (*Far and Near,* 1904), which
describes Yakutat Bay at the base of the Fairweather
coastal range, looming to heights well over fifteen thousand feet. While they did not see Mount Fairweather,
they did see the coastal range from the waist down,
wearing glaciers "like vast white aprons." The landscapes were for Burroughs vast and "astronomic";
perhaps the only way he could begin to get a handle on
trying to describe Alaska was in terms of the Catskills.
He writes: "One broad ice slope I recall which, with its
dark, straight lines of moraine dividing it into three
equal portions, suggested a side-hill farm in winter with
the tops of the stone walls showing above the snow. It
had a friendly, home look to me." And a bit later he
observes, "This part of the bay [Russell Fiord] is in size
like the Hudson and about sixty miles in length, but
how wild and savage!"

Here in Alaska Burroughs not only encountered
astronomic mountains and glaciers, but also (probably
for the first time) an Indian culture very much alive and
well, hunting seal and preparing meals of seal blubber
and cow parsnip. He also heard firsthand John Muir's
famous story of his experiences on a glacier with a brave
little dog called Stikeen (see John Muir's *Travels in
Alaska*). Ten years later John of the Birds would have
yet another outdoor adventure with John of the
Mountains.

"August Days" is a second selection from *Far and
Near* which takes us back to the banks of the Hudson
and Esopus rivers at the height of summer, when the
season has grown bold and aggressive and "flaunts her

weeds in our faces." Burroughs wishes to correct the
reader's poetic impressions of August by informing us
that it is not the season of the daisy, but that of the
orange hawkweed, not the season of the phoebe, but
that of the pewee and goldfinch. It is the time of the
fragrant horned bladderwort, and spiderwebs in the
grass. While not many songbirds sing, insects like
katydids and crickets make up for the loss. And in the
deep woods of August, mushrooms spread like
umbrellas in the rain or like more delicate Japanese
parasols. "August Days" reminds one, stylistically at
least, of "Spring Jottings," so thick are the observations and factual details.

And finally we have John of the Birds going west to
meet John of the Mountains again in the lyrical essay
"The Spell of the Yosemite," selected from *Time and
Change* (1912). In 1909 Burroughs, along with Clara
Barrus (his secretary and future biographer), met John
Muir and his daughter Helen to tour the Grand Canyon
of Arizona and the Yosemite Valley of California.
According to Barrus, Muir was as talkative as Uncle
Nathan of the Maine woods. He talked of his lonely
wanderings on mountains and glaciers, of his long walk
from Kentucky to the Gulf of Mexico, of bonny
Scotland, of storms, earthquakes, and waterfalls. When
the party first laid eyes on El Capitan guarding
Yosemite Valley, Barrus recalls, "Muir called out, How
does this compare with the Esopus Valley, Johnny?"
As if to answer this question in "The Spell of the
Yosemite," Burroughs writes, "The reader may create
for himself a good image of Yosemite by thinking of a
section of seven or eight miles of the Hudson River, midway of its course, as emptied of its water and deepened
three thousand feet or more, having the sides nearly vertical, with snow-white waterfalls fluttering against them

here and there, the famous spires and domes planted along the rim, and the landscape of groves and glades, with its still, clear winding river, occupying the bottom." Clearly Burroughs loved Yosemite Valley and its geological history, and surely he could have had no better guide than John Muir.

John Burroughs's nature writings are as accurate, vivid, and sensate as those of Henry David Thoreau and John Muir, and certainly he is in their tradition as a literary naturalist. Burroughs popularized the American "nature essay" in journals of wide circulation and helped establish it as a literary genre. Such a genre is at the leading edge of American literature today with such writers as Barry Lopez, Annie Dillard, John McPhee, and the late Edward Abbey. Surely all American nature writers owe some debt to John Burroughs who takes the reader along the trail and gives him the sight, sound and scent of the deep woods.

RICHARD F. FLECK
LARAMIE, WYOMING

THE ADIRONDACKS

WHEN I went to the Adirondacks, which was in the summer of 1863, I was in the first flush of my ornithological studies, and was curious, above all else, to know what birds I should find in these solitudes, — what new ones, and what ones already known to me.

In visiting vast, primitive, far-off woods one naturally expects to find something rare and precious, or something entirely new, but it commonly happens that one is disappointed. Thoreau made three excursions into the Maine woods, and, though he started the moose and caribou, had nothing more novel to report by way of bird notes than the songs of the wood thrush and the pewee. This was about my own experience in the Adirondacks. The birds for the most part prefer the vicinity of settlements and clearings, and it was at such places that I saw the greatest number and variety.

At the clearing of an old hunter and pioneer by the name of Hewett, where we paused a couple of days on first entering the woods, I saw many old friends and made some new acquaintances. The

snowbird was very abundant here, as it had been
at various points along the route after leaving Lake
George. As I went out to the spring in the morning to wash myself, a purple finch flew up before
me, having already performed its ablutions. I had
first observed this bird the winter before in the
Highlands of the Hudson, where, during several
clear but cold February mornings, a troop of them
sang most charmingly in a tree in front of my
house. The meeting with the bird here in its breeding haunts was a pleasant surprise. During the day
I observed several pine finches, — a dark brown
or brindlish bird, allied to the common yellowbird,
which it much resembles in its manner and habits.
They lingered familiarly about the house, sometimes alighting in a small tree within a few feet of
it. In one of the stumpy fields I saw an old favorite
in the grass finch or vesper sparrow. It was sitting
on a tall charred stub with food in its beak. But all
along the borders of the woods and in the bushy
parts of the fields there was a new song that I was
puzzled in tracing to the author. It was most noticeable in the morning and at twilight, but was
at all times singularly secret and elusive. I at last
discovered that it was the white-throated sparrow,
a common bird all through this region. Its song
is very delicate and plaintive, — a thin, wavering,
tremulous whistle, which disappoints one, however,
as it ends when it seems only to have begun. If the

bird could give us the finishing strain of which this seems only the prelude, it would stand first among feathered songsters.

By a little trout brook in a low part of the woods adjoining the clearing, I had a good time pursuing and identifying a number of warblers, — the speckled Canada, the black-throated blue, the yellow-rumped, and Audubon's warbler. The latter, which was leading its troop of young through a thick undergrowth on the banks of the creek where insects were plenty, was new to me.

It being August, the birds were all moulting, and sang only fitfully and by brief snatches. I remember hearing but one robin during the whole trip. This was by the Boreas River in the deep forest. It was like the voice of an old friend speaking my name.

From Hewett's, after engaging his youngest son, — the "Bub" of the family, — a young man about twenty and a thorough woodsman, as guide, we took to the woods in good earnest, our destination being the Stillwater of the Boreas, — a long, deep, dark reach in one of the remote branches of the Hudson, about six miles distant. Here we paused a couple of days, putting up in a dilapidated lumbermen's shanty, and cooking our fish over an old stove which had been left there. The most noteworthy incident of our stay at this point was the taking by myself of half a dozen splendid trout out of the Stillwater, after the guide had exhausted his art and his patience with very insignificant results. The place had a very trouty look; but as the season was late and the river warm, I knew the fish lay in deep water from which they could not be attracted. In deep water accordingly, and near the head of the hole, I determined to look for them. Securing a chub, I cut it into pieces about an inch long, and with these for bait sank my hook into the head of the Stillwater, and just to one side of the main current. In less than twenty minutes I had landed six noble fellows, three of them over one foot long each. The guide and my incredulous companions, who were watching me from the opposite shore, seeing my luck, whipped out their tackle in great haste and began casting first at a respectable distance from me, then all about me, but without a single catch. My own efforts suddenly became fruitless also, but I had conquered the guide, and thenceforth he treated me with the tone and freedom of a comrade and equal.

One afternoon we visited a cave some two miles down the stream, which had recently been discovered. We squeezed and wriggled through a big crack or cleft in the side of the mountain for about one hundred feet, when we emerged into a large dome-shaped passage, the abode, during certain seasons of the year, of innumerable bats, and at all times of primeval darkness. There were various other crannies and pit-holes opening into it, some of which we explored. The voice of running water was everywhere heard, betraying the proximity of the little stream by whose ceaseless corroding the cave and its entrance had been worn. This stream-let flowed out of the mouth of the cave, and came from a lake on the top of the mountain; this accounted for its warmth to the hand, which surprised us all.

Birds of any kind were rare in these woods. A pigeon hawk came prowling by our camp, and the faint piping call of the nuthatches, leading their young through the high trees, was often heard.

On the third day our guide proposed to conduct us to a lake in the mountains where we could float for deer.

Our journey commenced in a steep and rugged ascent, which brought us, after an hour's heavy climbing, to an elevated region of pine forest, years before ravished by lumbermen, and presenting all manner of obstacles to our awkward and incumbered pedestrianism. The woods were largely pine, though yellow birch, beech, and maple were common. The satisfaction of having a gun, should any game show itself, was the chief compensation to those of us who were thus burdened. A partridge would occasionally whir up before us, or a red squirrel snicker and hasten to his den; else the woods appeared quite tenantless. The most noted object was a mammoth pine, apparently the last of a great race, which presided over a cluster of yellow birches, on the side of the mountain.

About noon we came out upon a long, shallow sheet of water which the guide called Bloody-Moose Pond, from the tradition that a moose had been slaughtered there many years before. Looking out over the silent and lonely scene, his eye was the first to detect an object, apparently feeding upon lily-pads, which our willing fancies readily shaped into a deer. As we were eagerly waiting some movement to confirm this impression, it lifted up its head, and, lo! a great blue heron. Seeing us approach, it spread its long wings and flew solemnly across to a dead tree on the other side of the lake, enhancing rather than relieving the loneliness and desolation that brooded over the scene. As we proceeded, it flew from tree to tree in advance of us, apparently loth to be disturbed in its ancient and solitary domain. In the margin of the pond we found the pitcher-plant growing, and here and there in the sand the closed gentian lifted up its blue head.

In traversing the shores of this wild, desolate lake, I was conscious of a slight thrill of expectation, as if some secret of Nature might here be revealed, or some rare and unheard-of game disturbed. There is ever a lurking suspicion that the beginning of things is in some way associated with water, and one may notice that in his private walks he is led by a curious attraction to fetch all the springs and ponds in his route, as if by them was the place for wonders and miracles to happen. Once, while in advance of my companions, I saw, from a high rock, a commotion in the water near the shore, but on reaching the point found only the marks of a musquash.

Pressing on through the forest, after many adventures with the pine-knots, we reached, about the middle of the afternoon, our destination, Nate's Pond, — a pretty sheet of water, lying like a silver mirror in the lap of the mountain, about a mile long and half a mile wide, surrounded by dark forests of balsam, hemlock, and pine, and, like the one we had just passed, a very picture of unbroken solitude.

It is not in the woods alone to give one this impression of utter loneliness. In the woods are sounds and voices, and a dumb kind of companionship; one is little more than a walking tree himself; but come upon one of these mountain lakes, and the wildness stands revealed and meets you face to face. Water is thus facile and adaptive, that it makes the wild more wild, while it enhances culture and art.

The end of the pond which we approached was quite shoal, the stones rising above the surface as in a summer brook, and everywhere showing marks of the noble game we were in quest of, — footprints, dung, and cropped and uprooted lily-pads. After resting for a half hour, and replenishing our game-pouches at the expense of the most respectable frogs of the locality, we filed on through the soft, resinous pine-woods, intending to camp near the other end of the lake, where, the guide assured us, we should find a hunter's cabin ready built. A half-hour's march brought us to the locality, and a most delightful one it was, — so hospitable and inviting that all the kindly and beneficent influences of the woods must have abided there. In a slight depression in the woods, about one hundred yards from the lake, though hidden from it for a hunter's reasons, surrounded by a heavy growth of birch, hemlock, and pine, with a lining of balsam and fir, the rude cabin welcomed us. It was of the approved style, three sides inclosed, with a roof of bark and a bed of boughs, and a rock in front that afforded a permanent backlog to all fires. A faint voice of running water was heard near by, and, following the sound, a delicious spring rivulet was disclosed, hidden by the moss and débris as by a new fall of snow, but here and there rising in little well-like openings, as if for our special convenience. On smooth places on the logs I noticed female names inscribed in a female hand; and the guide told us of an English lady, an artist, who had traversed this region with a single guide, making sketches.

Our packs unslung and the kettle over, our first

move was to ascertain in what state of preservation
a certain dug-out might be, which, the guide averred,
he had left moored in the vicinity the summer
before, — for upon this hypothetical dug-out our
hopes of venison rested. After a little searching, it
was found under the top of a fallen hemlock, but in
a sorry condition. A large piece had been split out
of one end, and a fearful chink was visible nearly
to the water-line. Freed from the treetop, however,
and calked with a little moss, it floated with two
aboard, which was quite enough for our purpose.
A jack and an oar were necessary to complete the
arrangement, and before the sun had set our pro-
fessor of wood-craft had both in readiness. From
a young yellow birch an oar took shape with marvelous rapidity, — trimmed and smoothed with a
neatness almost fastidious, — no makeshift, but an
instrument fitted for the delicate work it was to
perform.

A jack was made with equal skill and speed. A
stout staff about three feet long was placed upright
in the bow of the boat, and held to its place by a
horizontal bar, through a hole in which it turned
easily: a half wheel eight or ten inches in diameter,
cut from a large chip, was placed at the top, around
which was bent a new section of birch bark, thus
forming a rude semicircular reflector. Three candles placed within the circle completed the jack.
With moss and boughs seats were arranged, — one

in the bow for the marksman, and one in the stern
for the oarsman. A meal of frogs and squirrels
was a good preparation, and, when darkness came,
all were keenly alive to the opportunity it brought.
Though by no means an expert in the use of the
gun, — adding the superlative degree of enthusiasm
to only the positive degree of skill, — yet it seemed
tacitly agreed that I should act as marksman and
kill the deer, if such was to be our luck.

After it was thoroughly dark, we went down to
make a short trial trip. Everything working to satisfaction, about ten o'clock we pushed out in earnest. For the twentieth time I felt in the pocket
that contained the matches, ran over the part I
was to perform, and pressed my gun firmly, to be
sure there was no mistake. My position was that
of kneeling directly under the jack, which I was to
light at the word. The night was clear, moonless,
and still. Nearing the middle of the lake, a breeze
from the west was barely perceptible, and noiselessly we glided before it. The guide handled his
oar with great dexterity; without lifting it from the
water or breaking the surface, he imparted the
steady, uniform motion desired. How silent it was!
The ear seemed the only sense, and to hold do-
minion over lake and forest. Occasionally a lily-
pad would brush along the bottom, and stooping
low I could hear a faint murmuring of the water
under the bow: else all was still. Then, almost as

by magic, we were encompassed by a huge black ring. The surface of the lake, when we had reached the centre, was slightly luminous from the starlight, and the dark, even forest-line that surrounded us, doubled by reflection in the water, presented a broad, unbroken belt of utter blackness. The effect was quite startling, like some huge conjurer's trick. It seemed as if we had crossed the boundary-line between the real and the imaginary, and this was indeed the land of shadows and of spectres. What magic oar was that the guide wielded that it could transport me to such a realm! Indeed, had I not committed some fatal mistake and left that trusty servant behind, and had not some wizard of the night stepped into his place? A slight splashing in-shore broke the spell and caused me to turn nervously to the oarsman: "Musquash," said he, and kept straight on.

Nearing the extreme end of the pond, the boat gently headed around, and silently we glided back into the clasp of that strange orbit. Slight sounds were heard as before, but nothing that indicated the presence of the game we were waiting for; and we reached the point of departure as innocent of venison as we had set out.

After an hour's delay, and near midnight, we pushed out again. My vigilance and susceptibility were rather sharpened than dulled by the waiting; and the features of the night had also deepened and

intensified. Night was at its meridian. The sky
had that soft luminousness which may often be observed near midnight at this season, and the "large
few stars" beamed mildly down. We floated out
into that spectral shadow-land and moved slowly on
as before. The silence was most impressive. Now
and then the faint *yeap* of some traveling bird
would come from the air overhead, or the wings
of a bat *whisp* quickly by, or an owl hoot off in
the mountains, giving to the silence and loneliness
a tongue. At short intervals some noise in-shore
would startle me, and cause me to turn inquiringly
to the silent figure in the stern.

The end of the lake was reached, and we turned
back. The novelty and the excitement began to
flag; tired nature began to assert her claims; the
movement was soothing, and the gunner slumbered
fitfully at his post. Presently something aroused
me. "There's a deer," whispered the guide. The
gun heard, and fairly jumped in my hand. Listening, there came the cracking of a limb, followed by
a sound as of something walking in shallow water.
It proceeded from the other end of the lake, over
against our camp. On we sped, noiselessly as ever,
but with increased velocity. Presently, with a thrill
of new intensity, I saw the boat was gradually
heading in that direction. Now, to a sportsman
who gets excited over a gray squirrel, and forgets
that he has a gun on the sudden appearance of a

fox, this was a severe trial. I felt suddenly cramped for room, and trimming the boat was out of the question. It seemed that I must make some noise in spite of myself. "Light the jack," said a soft whisper behind me. I fumbled nervously for a match, and dropped the first one. Another was drawn briskly across my knee and broke. A third lighted, but went out prematurely, in my haste to get it up to the jack. What would I not have given to see those wicks blaze! We were fast nearing the shore, — already the lily-pads began to brush along the bottom. Another attempt, and the light took. The gentle motion fanned the blaze, and in a moment a broad glare of light fell upon the water in front of us, while the boat remained in utter darkness.

By this time I had got beyond the nervous point, and had come round to perfect coolness and composure again, but preternaturally vigilant and keen. I was ready for any disclosures; not a sound was heard. In a few moments the trees alongshore were faintly visible. Every object put on the shape of a gigantic deer. A large rock looked just ready to bound away. The dry limbs of a prostrate tree were surely his antlers.

But what are those two luminous spots? Need the reader be told what they were? In a moment the head of a real deer became outlined; then his neck and foreshoulders; then his whole body. There he stood, up to his knees in the water, gazing fixedly at us, apparently arrested in the movement of putting his head down for a lily-pad, and evidently thinking it was some new-fangled moon sporting about there. "Let him have it," said my prompter, — and the crash came. There was a scuffle in the water, and a plunge in the woods. "He's gone," said I. "Wait a moment," said the guide, "and I will show you." Rapidly running the canoe ashore, we sprang out, and, holding the jack aloft, explored the vicinity by its light. There, over the logs and brush, I caught the glimmer of those luminous spots again. But, poor thing! there was little need of the second shot, which was the unkindest cut of all, for the deer had already fallen to the ground, and was fast expiring. The success was but a very indifferent one, after all, as the victim turned out to be only an old doe, upon whom maternal cares had evidently worn heavily during the summer.

This mode of taking deer is very novel and strange. The animal is evidently fascinated or bewildered. It does not appear to be frightened, but as if overwhelmed with amazement, or under the influence of some spell. It is not sufficiently master of the situation to be sensible of fear, or to think of escape by flight; and the experiment, to be successful, must be tried quickly, before the first feeling of bewilderment passes.

Witnessing the spectacle from the shore, I can conceive of nothing more sudden or astounding. You see no movement and hear no noise, but the light *grows* upon you, and stares and stares like a huge eye from the infernal regions.

According to the guide, when a deer has been played upon in this manner and escaped, he is not to be fooled a second time. Mounting the shore, he gives a long signal snort, which alarms every animal within hearing, and dashes away.

The sequel to the deer-shooting was a little sharp practice with a revolver upon a rabbit, or properly a hare, which was so taken with the spectacle of the camp-fire, and the sleeping figures lying about, that it ventured quite up in our midst; but while testing the quality of some condensed milk that sat uncovered at the foot of a large tree, poor Lepus had his spine injured by a bullet.

Those who lodge with Nature find early rising quite in order. It is our voluptuous beds, and isolation from the earth and the air, that prevents us from emulating the birds and beasts in this respect. With the citizen in his chamber, it is not morning, but breakfast-time. The camper-out, however, feels morning in the air, he smells it, sees it, hears it, and springs up with the general awakening. None were tardy at the row of white chips arranged on the trunk of a prostrate tree, when breakfast was halloed; for we were all anxious to try the venison. Few of us, however, took a second piece. It was black and strong.

The day was warm and calm, and we loafed at leisure. The woods were Nature's own. It was a luxury to ramble through them, — rank and shaggy and venerable, but with an aspect singularly ripe and mellow. No fire had consumed and no lumberman plundered. Every trunk and limb and leaf lay where it had fallen. At every step the foot sank into the moss, which, like a soft green snow, covered everything, making every stone a cushion and every rock a bed, — a grand old Norse parlor; adorned beyond art and upholstered beyond skill.

Indulging in a brief nap on a rug of club-moss carelessly dropped at the foot of a pine-tree, I woke up to find myself the subject of a discussion of a troop of chickadees. Presently three or four shy wood warblers came to look upon this strange creature that had wandered into their haunts; else I passed quite unnoticed.

By the lake, I met that orchard beauty, the cedar waxwing, spending his vacation in the assumed character of a flycatcher, whose part he performed with great accuracy and deliberation. Only a month before I had seen him regaling himself upon cherries in the garden and orchard; but as the dog-days approached he set out for the streams and lakes, to divert himself with the more exciting pursuits of the chase. From the tops of the dead trees along the border of the lake, he would sally out in all directions, sweeping through long curves, alternately mounting and descending, now reaching up for a fly high in air, now sinking low for one near the surface, and returning to his perch in a few moments for a fresh start.

The pine finch was also here, though, as usual, never appearing at home, but with a waiting, expectant air. Here also I met my beautiful singer, the hermit thrush, but with no song in his throat now. A week or two later and he was on his journey southward. This was the only species of thrush I saw in the Adirondacks. Near Lake Sandford, where were large tracts of raspberry and wild cherry, I saw numbers of them. A boy whom we met, driving home some stray cows, said it was the "partridge-bird," no doubt from the resemblance of its note, when disturbed, to the cluck of the partridge.

Nate's Pond contained perch and sunfish but no trout. Its water was not pure enough for trout. Was there ever any other fish so fastidious as this, requiring such sweet harmony and perfection of the elements for its production and sustenance? On higher ground about a mile distant was a trout pond, the shores of which were steep and rocky.

Our next move was a tramp of about twelve miles

through the wilderness, most of the way in a drenching rain, to a place called the Lower Iron Works,
situated on the road leading in to Long Lake, which
is about a day's drive farther on. We found a comfortable hotel here, and were glad enough to avail
ourselves of the shelter and warmth which it offered. There was a little settlement and some quite
good farms. The place commands a fine view to
the north of Indian Pass, Mount Marcy, and the
adjacent mountains. On the afternoon of our arrival, and also the next morning, the view was completely shut off by the fog. But about the middle of
the forenoon the wind changed, the fog lifted, and
revealed to us the grandest mountain scenery we
had beheld on our journey. There they sat about
fifteen miles distant, a group of them, — Mount
Marcy, Mount McIntyre, and Mount Golden, the
real Adirondack monarchs. It was an impressive
sight, rendered doubly so by the sudden manner
in which it was revealed to us by that scene-shifter
the Wind.

I saw blackbirds at this place, and sparrows, and
the solitary sandpiper, and the Canada woodpecker,
and, a large number of hummingbirds. Indeed, I
saw more of the latter here than I ever before saw
in any one locality. Their squeaking and whirring
were almost incessant.

The Adirondack Iron Works belong to the past.
Over thirty years ago a company in Jersey City

purchased some sixty thousand acres of land lying along the Adirondack River, and abounding in magnetic iron ore. The land was cleared, roads, dams, and forges constructed, and the work of manufacturing iron begun.

At this point a dam was built across the Hudson, the waters of which flowed back into Lake Sandford, about five miles above. The lake itself being some six miles long, tolerable navigation was thus established for a distance of eleven miles, to the Upper Works, which seem to have been the only works in operation. At the Lower Works, besides the remains of the dam, the only vestige I saw was a long low mound, overgrown with grass and weeds, that suggested a rude earthwork. We were told that it was once a pile of wood containing hundreds of cords, cut in regular lengths and corded up here for use in the furnaces.

At the Upper Works, some twelve miles distant, quite a village had been built, which was now entirely abandoned, with the exception of a single family.

A march to this place was our next undertaking. The road for two or three miles kept up from the river and led us by three or four rough, stumpy farms. It then approached the lake and kept along its shores. It was here a dilapidated corduroy structure that compelled the traveler to keep an eye on his feet. Blue jays, two or three small hawks,

a solitary wild pigeon, and ruffed grouse were seen
along the route. Now and then the lake gleamed
through the trees, or we crossed on a shaky bridge
some of its arms or inlets. After a while we began
to pass dilapidated houses by the roadside. One
little frame house I remembered particularly; the
door was off the hinges and leaned against the
jambs, the windows had but a few panes left, which
glared vacantly. The yard and little garden spot
were overrun with a heavy growth of timothy, and
the fences had all long since gone to decay. At
the head of the lake a large stone building projected
from the steep bank and extended over the road.
A little beyond, the valley opened to the east, and
looking ahead about one mile we saw smoke going
up from a single chimney. Pressing on, just as the
sun was setting we entered the deserted village.
The barking of the dog brought the whole family
into the street, and they stood till we came up.
Strangers in that country were a novelty, and we
were greeted like familiar acquaintances.

Hunter, the head, proved to be a first-rate type
of an Americanized Irishman. His wife was a
Scotch woman. They had a family of five or six
children, two of them grown-up daughters, — modest, comely young women as you would find anywhere. The elder of the two had spent a winter in
New York with her aunt, which perhaps made her
a little more self-conscious when in the presence of

the strange young men. Hunter was hired by the company at a dollar a day to live here and see that things were not wantonly destroyed, but allowed to go to decay properly and decently. He had a substantial roomy frame house and any amount of grass and woodland. He had good barns and kept considerable stock, and raised various farm products, but only for his own use, as the difficulties of transportation to market some seventy miles distant made it no object. He usually went to Ticonderoga on Lake Champlain once a year for his groceries, etc. His post-office was twelve miles below at the Lower Works, where the mail passed twice a week. There was not a doctor, or lawyer, or preacher within twenty-five miles. In winter, months elapse without their seeing anybody from the outside world. In summer, parties occasionally pass through here on their way to Indian Pass and Mount Marcy. Hundreds of tons of good timothy hay annually rot down upon the cleared land.

After nightfall we went out and walked up and down the grass-grown streets. It was a curious and melancholy spectacle. The remoteness and surrounding wildness rendered the scene doubly impressive. And the next day and the next the place was an object of wonder. There were about thirty buildings in all, most of them small frame houses with a door and two windows opening into a small yard in front and a garden in the rear, such as are

usually occupied by the laborers in a country manufacturing district. There was one large two-story
boarding-house, a schoolhouse with a cupola and
a bell in it, and numerous sheds and forges, and a
saw-mill. In front of the saw-mill, and ready to
be rolled to their place on the carriage, lay a large
pile of pine logs, so decayed that one could run his
walking-stick through them. Near by, a building
filled with charcoal was bursting open and the coal
going to waste on the ground. The smelting works
were also much crumbled by time. The schoolhouse was still used. Every day one of the daughters
assembles her smaller brothers and sisters there
and school keeps. The district library contained
nearly one hundred readable books, which were
well thumbed.

The absence of society had made the family all
good readers. We brought them an illustrated
newspaper which was awaiting them in the post-
office at the Lower Works. It was read and reread
with great eagerness by every member of the house-
hold.

The iron ore cropped out on every hand. There
was apparently mountains of it; one could see it in
the stones along the road. But the difficulties met
with in separating the iron from its alloys, together
with the expense of transportation and the failure
of certain railroad schemes, caused the works to be
abandoned. No doubt the time is not distant when

these obstacles will be overcome and this region reopened.

At present it is an admirable place to go to. There is fishing and hunting and boating and mountain-climbing within easy reach, and a good roof over your head at night, which is no small matter. One is often disqualified for enjoying the woods after he gets there by the loss of sleep and of proper food taken at seasonable times. This point attended to, one is in the humor for any enterprise.

About half a mile northeast of the village is Lake Henderson, a very irregular and picturesque sheet of water, surrounded by dark evergreen forests, and abutted by two or three bold promontories with mottled white and gray rocks. Its greatest extent in any one direction is perhaps less than a mile. Its waters are perfectly clear and abound in lake trout. A considerable stream flows into it, which comes down from Indian Pass.

A mile south of the village is Lake Sandford. This is a more open and exposed sheet of water and much larger. From some parts of it Mount Marcy and the gorge of the Indian Pass are seen to excellent advantage. The Indian Pass shows as a huge cleft in the mountain, the gray walls rising on one side perpendicularly for many hundred feet. This lake abounds in white and yellow perch and in pickerel ; of the latter single specimens are often caught which weigh fifteen pounds. There were a few wild ducks on both lakes. A brood of the goosander or red merganser, the young not yet able to fly, were the occasion of some spirited rowing. But with two pairs of oars in a trim light skiff, it was impossible to come up with them. Yet we could not resist the temptation to give them a chase every day when we first came on the lake. It needed a good long pull to sober us down so we could fish.

The land on the east side of the lake had been burnt over, and was now mostly grown up with wild cherry and red raspberry bushes. Ruffed grouse were found here in great numbers. The Canada grouse was also common. I shot eight of the latter in less than an hour on one occasion; the eighth one, which was an old male, was killed with smooth pebble-stones, my shot having run short. The wounded bird ran under a pile of brush, like a frightened hen. Thrusting a forked stick down through the interstices, I soon stopped his breathing. Wild pigeons were quite numerous also. These latter recall a singular freak of the sharp-shinned hawk. A flock of pigeons alighted on the top of a dead hemlock standing in the edge of a swamp. I got over the fence and moved toward them across an open space. I had not taken many steps when, on looking up, I saw the whole flock again in motion flying very rapidly around the butt of a hill. Just then this hawk alighted on the same tree. I stepped back into the road and paused a moment, in doubt which course to go. At that instant the little hawk launched into the air and came as straight as an arrow toward me. I looked in amazement, but in less than half a minute he was within fifty feet of my face, coming full tilt as if he had sighted my nose. Almost in self-defense I let fly one barrel of my gun, and the mangled form of the audacious marauder fell literally between my feet.

Of wild animals, such as bears, panthers, wolves, wildcats, etc., we neither saw nor heard any in the Adirondacks. "A howling wilderness," Thoreau says, "seldom ever howls. The howling is chiefly done by the imagination of the traveler." Hunter said he often saw bear-tracks in the snow, but had never yet met Bruin. Deer are more or less abundant everywhere, and one old sportsman declares there is yet a single moose in these mountains. On our return, a pioneer settler, at whose house we stayed overnight, told us a long adventure he had had with a panther. He related how it screamed, how it followed him in the brush, how he took to his boat, how its eyes gleamed from the shore, and how he fired his rifle at them with fatal effect. His wife in the mean time took something from a drawer, and, as her husband finished his recital, she produced a toe-nail of the identical animal with marked dramatic effect.

But better than fish or game or grand scenery, or

any adventure by night or day, is the wordless intercourse with rude Nature one has on these expeditions. It is something to press the pulse of our old mother by mountain lakes and streams, and know what health and vigor are in her veins, and how regardless of observation she deports herself.

1866.

BIRCH BROWSINGS

THE region of which I am about to speak lies in the southern part of the State of New York, and comprises parts of three counties, — Ulster, Sullivan, and Delaware. It is drained by tributaries of both the Hudson and Delaware, and, next to the Adirondack section, contains more wild land than any other tract in the State. The mountains which traverse it, and impart to it its severe northern climate, belong properly to the Catskill range. On some maps of the State they are called the Pine Mountains, though with obvious local impropriety, as pine, so far as I have observed, is nowhere found upon them. "Birch Mountains" would be a more characteristic name, as on their summits birch is the prevailing tree. They are the natural home of the black and yellow birch, which grow here to unusual size. On their sides beech and maple abound; while, mantling their lower slopes and darkening the valleys, hemlock formerly enticed the lumberman and tanner. Except in remote or inaccessible localities, the latter tree is now almost never found. In Shandaken and along the Esopus

it is about the only product the country yielded, or
is likely to yield. Tanneries by the score have
arisen and flourished upon the bark, and some of
them still remain. Passing through that region the
present season, I saw that the few patches of hemlock that still lingered high up on the sides of the
mountains were being felled and peeled, the fresh
white boles of the trees, just stripped of their bark,
being visible a long distance.

Among these mountains there are no sharp peaks,
or abrupt declivities, as in a volcanic region, but
long, uniform ranges, heavily timbered to their summits, and delighting the eye with vast, undulating
horizon lines. Looking south from the heights about
the head of the Delaware, one sees, twenty miles
away, a continual succession of blue ranges, one
behind the other. If a few large trees are missing
on the sky line, one can see the break a long distance off.

Approaching this region from the Hudson River
side, you cross a rough, rolling stretch of country,
skirting the base of the Catskills, which from a
point near Saugerties sweep inland; after a drive
of a few hours you are within the shadow of a high,
bold mountain, which forms a sort of butt-end to
this part of the range, and which is simply called
High Point. To the east and southeast it slopes
down rapidly to the plain, and looks defiance toward
the Hudson, twenty miles distant; in the rear of

it, and radiating from it west and northwest, are
numerous smaller ranges, backing up, as it were,
this haughty chief.

From this point through to Pennsylvania, a distance of nearly one hundred miles, stretches the
tract of which I speak. It is a belt of country from
twenty to thirty miles wide, bleak and wild, and
but sparsely settled. The traveler on the New
York and Erie Railroad gets a glimpse of it.

Many cold, rapid trout streams, which flow to
all points of the compass, have their source in the
small lakes and copious mountain springs of this
region. The names of some of them are Mill Brook,
Dry Brook, Willewemack, Beaver Kill, Elk Bush
Kill, Panther Kill, Neversink, Big Ingin, and
Callikoon. Beaver Kill is the main outlet on the
west. It joins the Delaware in the wilds of Han-
cock. The Neversink lays open the region to the
south, and also joins the Delaware. To the east,
various Kills unite with the Big Ingin to form the
Esopus, which flows into the Hudson. Dry Brook
and Mill Brook, both famous trout streams, from
twelve to fifteen miles long, find their way into the
Delaware.

The east or Pepacton branch of the Delaware
itself takes its rise near here in a deep pass between
the mountains. I have many times drunk at a
copious spring by the roadside, where the infant
river first sees the light. A few yards beyond, the

water flows the other way, directing its course through the Bear Kill and Schoharie Kill into the Mohawk.

Such game and wild animals as still linger in the State are found in this region. Bears occasionally make havoc among the sheep. The clearings at the head of a valley are oftenest the scene of their depredations.

Wild pigeons, in immense numbers, used to breed regularly in the valley of the Big Ingin and about the head of the Neversink. The treetops for miles were full of their nests, while the going and coming of the old birds kept up a constant din. But the gunners soon got wind of it, and from far and near were wont to pour in during the spring, and to slaughter both old and young. This practice soon had the effect of driving the pigeons all away, and now only a few pairs breed in these woods.

Deer are still met with, though they are becoming scarcer every year. Last winter near seventy head were killed on the Beaver Kill alone. I heard of one wretch, who, finding the deer snowbound, walked up to them on his snowshoes, and one morning before breakfast slaughtered six, leaving their carcasses where they fell. There are traditions of persons having been smitten blind or senseless when about to commit some heinous offense, but the fact that this villain escaped without some such visitation throws discredit on all such stories.

The great attraction, however, of this region, is the brook trout, with which the streams and lakes abound. The water is of excessive coldness, the thermometer indicating 44° and 45° in the springs, and 47° or 48° in the smaller streams. The trout are generally small, but in the more remote branches their number is very great. In such localities the fish are quite black, but in the lakes they are of a lustre and brilliancy impossible to describe.

These waters have been much visited of late years by fishing parties, and the name of Beaver Kill is now a potent word among New York sportsmen.

One lake, in the wilds of Callikoon, abounds in a peculiar species of white sucker, which is of excellent quality. It is taken only in spring, during the spawning season, at the time "when the leaves are as big as a chipmunk's ears." The fish run up the small streams and inlets, beginning at nightfall, and continuing till the channel is literally packed with them, and every inch of space is occupied. The fishermen pounce upon them at such times, and scoop them up by the bushel, usually wading right into the living mass and landing the fish with their hands. A small party will often secure in this manner a wagon-load of fish. Certain conditions of the weather, as a warm south or southwest wind, are considered most favorable for the fish to run.

Though familiar all my life with the outskirts of this region, I have only twice dipped into its wilder

portions. Once in 1860 a friend and myself traced
the Beaver Kill to its source, and encamped by
Balsam Lake. A cold and protracted rainstorm
coming on, we were obliged to leave the woods before we were ready. Neither of us will soon forget
that tramp by an unknown route over the mountains, encumbered as we were with a hundred and
one superfluities which we had foolishly brought
along to solace ourselves with in the woods ; nor
that halt on the summit, where we cooked and ate
our fish in a drizzling rain; nor, again, that rude
log house, with its sweet hospitality, which we
reached just at nightfall on Mill Brook.

In 1868 a party of three of us set out for a brief
trouting excursion to a body of water called Thomas's
Lake, situated in the same chain of mountains.
On this excursion, more particularly than on any
other I have ever undertaken, I was taught how
poor an Indian I should make, and what a ridiculous figure a party of men may cut in the woods
when the way is uncertain and the mountains high.

We left our team at a farmhouse near the head
of the Mill Brook, one June afternoon, and with
knapsacks on our shoulders struck into the woods
at the base of the mountain, hoping to cross the
range that intervened between us and the lake by
sunset. We engaged a good-natured but rather
indolent young man, who happened to be stopping
at the house, and who had carried a knapsack in

the Union armies, to pilot us a couple of miles
into the woods so as to guard against any mistakes
at the outset. It seemed the easiest thing in the
world to find the lake. The lay of the land was so
simple, according to accounts, that I felt sure I
could go to it in the dark. "Go up this little brook
to its source on the side of the mountain," they
said. "The valley that contains the lake heads
directly on the other side." What could be easier!
But on a little further inquiry, they said we should
"bear well to the left" when we reached the top of
the mountain. This opened the doors again; "bearing well to the left" was an uncertain performance in strange woods. We might bear so well to
the left that it would bring us ill. But why bear
to the left at all, if the lake was directly opposite?
Well, not quite opposite; a little to the left. There
were two or three other valleys that headed in near
there. We could easily find the right one. But to
make assurance doubly sure, we engaged a guide,
as stated, to give us a good start, and go with us
beyond the bearing-to-the-left point. He had been
to the lake the winter before and knew the way.
Our course, the first half hour, was along an obscure
wood-road which had been used for drawing ash
logs off the mountain in winter. There was some
hemlock, but more maple and birch. The woods
were dense and free from underbrush, the ascent
gradual. Most of the way we kept the voice of the

creek in our ear on the right. I approached it once, and found it swarming with trout. The water was as cold as one ever need wish. After a while the ascent grew steeper, the creek became a mere rill that issued from beneath loose, moss-covered rocks and stones, and with much labor and puffing we drew ourselves up the rugged declivity. Every mountain has its steepest point, which is usually near the summit, in keeping, I suppose, with the providence that makes the darkest hour just before day. It is steep, steeper, steepest, till you emerge on the smooth level or gently rounded space at the top, which the old ice-gods polished off so long ago.

We found this mountain had a hollow in its back where the ground was soft and swampy. Some gigantic ferns, which we passed through, came nearly to our shoulders. We passed also several patches of swamp honeysuckles, red with blossoms.

Our guide at length paused on a big rock where the land began to dip down the other way, and concluded that he had gone far enough, and that we would now have no difficulty in finding the lake. "It must lie right down there," he said, pointing with his hand. But it was plain that he was not quite sure in his own mind. He had several times wavered in his course, and had shown considerable embarrassment when bearing to the left across the summit. Still we thought little of it. We were full of confidence, and, bidding him adieu, plunged down the mountain-side, following a spring run that we had no doubt led to the lake.

In these woods, which had a southeastern exposure, I first began to notice the wood thrush. In coming up the other side I had not seen a feather of any kind, or heard a note. Now the golden *trillide-de* of the wood thrush sounded through the silent woods. While looking for a fish-pole about halfway down the mountain, I saw a thrush's nest in a little sapling about ten feet from the ground.

After continuing our descent till our only guide, the spring run, became quite a trout brook, and its tiny murmur a loud brawl, we began to peer anxiously through the trees for a glimpse of the lake, or for some conformation of the land that would indicate its proximity. An object which we vaguely discerned in looking under the near trees and over the more distant ones proved, on further inspection, to be a patch of plowed ground. Presently we made out a burnt fallow near it. This was a wet blanket to our enthusiasm. No lake, no sport, no trout for supper that night. The rather indolent young man had either played us a trick, or, as seemed more likely, had missed the way. We were particularly anxious to be at the lake between sundown and dark, as at that time the trout jump most freely.

Pushing on, we soon emerged into a stumpy field, at the head of a steep valley, which swept around toward the west. About two hundred rods below us was a rude log house, with smoke issuing from the chimney. A boy came out and moved toward the spring with a pail in his hand. We shouted to him, when he turned and ran back into the house without pausing to reply. In a moment the whole family hastily rushed into the yard, and turned their faces toward us. If we had come down their chimney, they could not have seemed more astonished. Not making out what they said, I went down to the house, and learned to my chagrin that we were still on the Mill Brook side, having crossed only a spur of the mountain. We had not borne sufficiently to the left, so that the main range, which, at the point of crossing, suddenly breaks off to the southeast, still intervened between us and the lake. We were about five miles, as the water runs, from the point of starting, and over two from the lake. We must go directly back to the top of the range where the guide had left us, and then, by keeping well to the left, we would soon come to a line of marked trees, which would lead us to the lake. So, turning upon our trail, we doggedly began the work of undoing what we had just done, — in all cases a disagreeable task, in this case a very laborious one also. It was after sunset when we turned back, and before we had got halfway up the mountain, it began to be quite dark. We were often obliged to rest our packs against trees and take breath, which made our progress slow. Finally a halt was called, beside an immense flat rock which had paused on its slide down the mountain, and we prepared to encamp for the night. A fire was built, the rock cleared off, a small ration of bread served out, our accoutrements hung up out of the way of the hedgehogs that were supposed to infest the locality, and then we disposed ourselves for sleep. If the owls or porcupines (and I think I heard one of the latter in the middle of the night) reconnoitred our camp, they saw a buffalo robe spread upon a rock, with three old felt hats arranged on one side, and three pairs of sorry-looking cowhide boots protruding from the other.

When we lay down, there was apparently not a mosquito in the woods; but the "no-see-ems," as Thoreau's Indian aptly named the midges, soon found us out, and after the fire had gone down, annoyed us much. My hands and wrists suddenly began to smart and itch in a most unaccountable manner. My first thought was that they had been poisoned in some way. Then the smarting extended to my neck and face, even to my scalp, when I began to suspect what was the matter. So, wrapping myself up more thoroughly, and stowing my hands away as best I could, I tried to sleep, being some time behind my companions, who appeared not to mind the "no-see-ems." I was further annoyed by some little irregularity on my side of the couch. The chambermaid had not beaten it up well. One huge lump refused to be mollified, and each attempt to adapt it to some natural hollow in my own body brought only a moment's relief. But at last I got the better of this also and slept. Late in the night I woke up, just in time to hear a golden-crowned thrush sing in a tree near by. It sang as loud and cheerily as at midday, and I thought myself, after all, quite in luck. Birds occasionally sing at night, just as the cock crows. I have heard the hairbird, and the note of the kingbird ; and the ruffed grouse frequently drums at night.

At the first faint signs of day a wood thrush sang, a few rods below us. Then after a little delay, as the gray light began to grow around, thrushes broke out in full song in all parts of the woods. I thought I had never before heard them sing so sweetly. Such a leisurely, golden chant! — it consoled us for all we had undergone. It was the first thing in order, — the worms were safe till after this morning chorus. I judged that the birds roosted but a few feet from the ground. In fact, a bird in all cases roosts where it builds, and the wood thrush occupies, as it were, the first story of the woods.

There is something singular about the distribution of the wood thrushes. At an earlier stage of my observations I should have been much surprised at finding them in these woods. Indeed, I had stated

in print on two occasions that the wood thrush was
not found in the higher lands of the Catskills, but
that the hermit thrush and the veery, or Wilson's
thrush, were common. It turns out that the statement is only half true. The wood thrush is found
also, but is much more rare and secluded in its habits than either of the others, being seen only during
the breeding season on remote mountains, and then
only on their eastern and southern slopes. I have
never yet in this region found the bird spending
the season in the near and familiar woods, which is
directly contrary to observations I have made in
other parts of the State. So different are the habits of birds in different localities.

As soon as it was fairly light we were up and
ready to resume our march. A small bit of bread
and butter and a swallow or two of whiskey was all
we had for breakfast that morning. Our supply of
each was very limited, and we were anxious to save
a little of both, to relieve the diet of trout to which
we looked forward.

At an early hour we reached the rock where we
had parted with the guide, and looked around us
into the dense, trackless woods with many misgiv-
ings. To strike out now on our own hook, where
the way was so blind and after the experience we
had just had, was a step not to be carelessly taken.
The tops of these mountains are so broad, and a
short distance in the woods seems so far, that one

is by no means master of the situation after reaching the summit. And then there are so many spurs and offshoots and changes of direction, added to the impossibility of making any generalization by the aid of the eye, that before one is aware of it he is very wide of his mark.

I remembered now that a young farmer of my acquaintance had told me how he had made a long day's march through the heart of this region, without path or guide of any kind, and had hit his mark squarely. He had been barkpeeling in Callikoon, — a famous country for bark, — and, having got enough of it, he desired to reach his home on Dry Brook without making the usual circuitous journey between the two places. To do this necessitated a march of ten or twelve miles across several ranges of mountains and through an unbroken forest, — a hazardous undertaking in which no one would join him. Even the old hunters who were familiar with the ground dissuaded him and predicted the failure of his enterprise. But having made up his mind, he possessed himself thoroughly of the topography of the country from the aforesaid hunters, shouldered his axe, and set out, holding a straight course through the woods, and turning aside for neither swamps, streams, nor mountains. When he paused to rest he would mark some object ahead of him with his eye, in order that on getting up again he might not deviate from his course. His directors had told him of a hunter's cabin about midway on his route, which if he struck he might be sure he was right. About noon this cabin was reached, and at sunset he emerged at the head of Dry Brook.

After looking in vain for the line of marked trees, we moved off to the left in a doubtful, hesitating manner, keeping on the highest ground and blazing the trees as we went. We were afraid to go downhill, lest we should descend too soon; our vantage-ground was high ground. A thick fog coming on, we were more bewildered than ever. Still we pressed forward, climbing up ledges and wading through ferns for about two hours, when we paused by a spring that issued from beneath an immense wall of rock that belted the highest part of the mountain. There was quite a broad plateau here, and the birch wood was very dense, and the trees of unusual size.

After resting and exchanging opinions, we all concluded that it was best not to continue our search encumbered as we were; but we were not willing to abandon it altogether, and I proposed to my companions to leave them beside the spring with our traps, while I made one thorough and final effort to find the lake. If I succeeded and desired them to come forward, I was to fire my gun three times; if I failed and wished to return, I would fire it twice, they of course responding.

So, filling my canteen from the spring, I set out again, taking the spring run for my guide. Before I had followed it two hundred yards, it sank into the ground at my feet. I had half a mind to be superstitious and to believe that we were under a spell, since our guides played us such tricks. However, I determined to put the matter to a further test, and struck out boldly to the left. This seemed to be the keyword, — to the left, to the left. The fog had now lifted, so that I could form a better idea of the lay of the land. Twice I looked down the steep sides of the mountain, sorely tempted to risk a plunge. Still I hesitated and kept along on the brink. As I stood on a rock deliberating, I heard a crackling of the brush, like the tread of some large game, on a plateau below me. Suspecting the truth of the case, I moved stealthily down, and found a herd of young cattle leisurely browsing. We had several times crossed their trail, and had seen that morning a level, grassy place on the top of the mountain, where they had passed the night. Instead of being frightened, as I had expected, they seemed greatly delighted, and gathered around me as if to inquire the tidings from the outer world, — perhaps the quotations of the cattle market. They came up to me, and eagerly licked my hand, clothes, and gun. Salt was what they were after, and they were ready to swallow anything that contained the smallest percentage of it. They were mostly yearlings and as sleek as moles. They had a very gamy look. We were afterwards told that, in the spring, the farmers round about turn into these woods their young cattle, which do not come out again till fall. They are then in good condition, — not fat, like grass-fed cattle, but trim and supple, like deer. Once a month the owner hunts them up and salts them. They have their beats, and seldom wander beyond well-defined limits. It was interesting to see them feed. They browsed on the low limbs and bushes, and on the various plants, munching at everything without any apparent discrimination.

They attempted to follow me, but I escaped them by clambering down some steep rocks. I now found myself gradually edging down the side of the mountain, keeping around it in a spiral manner, and scanning the woods and the shape of the ground for some encouraging hint or sign. Finally the woods became more open, and the descent less rapid. The trees were remarkably straight and uniform in size. Black birches, the first I had seen, were very numerous. I felt encouraged. Listening attentively, I caught, from a breeze just lifting the drooping leaves, a sound that I willingly believed was made by a bullfrog. On this hint, I tore down through the woods at my highest speed. Then I paused and listened again. This time there was no mistaking it ; it was the sound of frogs. Much elated, I rushed on. By and by I could hear them as I ran. *Pthrung, pthrung*, croaked the old ones; *pug, pug*, shrilly joined in the smaller fry.

Then I caught, through the lower trees, a gleam of blue, which I first thought was distant sky. A second look and I knew it to be water, and in a moment more I stepped from the woods and stood upon the shore of the lake. I exulted silently. There it was at last, sparkling in the morning sun, and as beautiful as a dream. It was so good to come upon such open space and such bright hues, after wandering in the dim, dense woods! The eye is as delighted as an escaped bird, and darts gleefully from point to point.

The lake was a long oval, scarcely more than a mile in circumference, with evenly wooded shores, which rose gradually on all sides. After contemplating the scene for a moment, I stepped back into the woods, and, loading my gun as heavily as I dared, discharged it three times. The reports seemed to fill all the mountains with sound. The frogs quickly hushed, and I listened for the response. But no response came. Then I tried again and again, but without evoking an answer. One of my companions, however, who had climbed to the top of the high rocks in the rear of the spring, thought he heard faintly one report. It seemed an immense distance below him, and far around under the mountain. I knew I had come a long way, and hardly expected to be able to communicate with my companions in the manner agreed upon. I therefore started back, choosing my course without any reference to the circuitous route by which I had come, and loading heavily and firing at intervals. I must have aroused many long-dormant echoes from a Rip Van Winkle sleep. As my powder got low, I fired and halloed alternately, till I came near splitting both my throat and gun. Finally, after I had begun to have a very ugly feeling of alarm and disappointment, and to cast about vaguely for some course to pursue in the emergency that seemed near at hand, — namely, the loss of my companions now I had found the lake, — a favoring breeze brought me the last echo of a response. I rejoined with spirit, and hastened with all speed in the direction whence the sound had come, but, after repeated trials, failed to elicit another answering sound. This filled me with apprehension again. I feared that my friends had been misled by the reverberations, and I pictured them to myself hastening in the opposite direction. Paying little attention to my course, but paying dearly for my carelessness afterward, I rushed forward to undeceive them. But they had not been deceived, and in a few moments an answering shout revealed them near at hand. I heard their tramp, the bushes parted, and we three met again.

In answer to their eager inquiries, I assured them that I had seen the lake, that it was at the foot of the mountain, and that we could not miss it if we kept straight down from where we then were.

My clothes were soaked with perspiration, but I shouldered my knapsack with alacrity, and we began the descent. I noticed that the woods were much thicker, and had quite a different look from those I had passed through, but thought nothing of it, as I expected to strike the lake near its head, whereas I had before come out at its foot. We had not gone far when we crossed a line of marked trees, which my companions were disposed to follow. It intersected our course nearly at right angles, and kept along and up the side of the mountain. My impression was that it led up from the lake, and that by keeping our own course we should reach the lake sooner than if we followed this line.

About halfway down the mountain, we could see through the interstices the opposite slope. I encouraged my comrades by telling them that the lake was between us and that, and not more than half a mile distant. We soon reached the bottom, where we found a small stream and quite an extensive alder swamp, evidently the ancient bed of a lake. I explained to my half-vexed and half-incredulous companions that we were probably above the lake, and that this stream must lead to it. "Follow it," they said; "we will wait here till we hear from you."

So I went on, more than ever disposed to believe

that we were under a spell, and that the lake had
slipped from my grasp after all. Seeing no favorable sign as I went forward, I laid down my accoutrements, and climbed a decayed beech that leaned
out over the swamp and promised a good view from
the top. As I stretched myself up to look around
from the highest attainable branch, there was suddenly a loud crack at the root. With a celerity
that would at least have done credit to a bear, I
regained the ground, having caught but a momen-
tary glimpse of the country, but enough to convince
me no lake was near. Leaving all incumbrances
here but my gun, I still pressed on, loath to be thus
baffled. After floundering through another alder
swamp for nearly half a mile, I flattered myself
that I was close on to the lake. I caught sight of
a low spur of the mountain sweeping around like
a half-extended arm, and I fondly imagined that
within its clasp was the object of my search. But
I found only more alder swamp. After this region
was cleared, the creek began to descend the mountain very rapidly. Its banks became high and narrow, and it went whirling away with a sound that
seemed to my ears like a burst of ironical laughter. I turned back with a feeling of mingled dis-
gust, shame, and vexation. In fact I was almost
sick, and when I reached my companions, after an
absence of nearly two hours, hungry, fatigued, and
disheartened, I would have sold my interest in

Thomas's Lake at a very low figure. For the first time, I heartily wished myself well out of the woods. Thomas might keep his lake, and the enchanters guard his possession! I doubted if he had ever found it the second time, or if any one else ever had.

My companions, who were quite fresh, and who had not felt the strain of baffled purpose as I had, assumed a more encouraging tone. After I had rested awhile, and partaken sparingly of the bread and whiskey, which in such an emergency is a great improvement on bread and water, I agreed to their proposition that we should make another attempt. As if to reassure us, a robin sounded his cheery call near by, and the winter wren, the first I had heard in these woods, set his music-box going, which fairly ran over with fine, gushing, lyrical sounds. There can be no doubt but this bird is one of our finest songsters. If it would only thrive and sing well when caged, like the canary, how far it would surpass that bird! It has all the vivacity and versatility of the canary, without any of its shrillness. Its song is indeed a little cascade of melody.

We again retraced our steps, rolling the stone, as it were, back up the mountain, determined to commit ourselves to the line of marked trees. These we finally reached, and, after exploring the country to the right, saw that bearing to the left was still the order. The trail led up over a gentle rise of ground, and in less than twenty minutes we were in the woods I had passed through when I found the lake. The error I had made was then plain: we had come off the mountain a few paces too far to the right, and so had passed down on the wrong side of the ridge, into what we afterwards learned was the valley of Alder Creek.

We now made good time, and before many minutes I again saw the mimic sky glance through the trees. As we approached the lake, a solitary woodchuck, the first wild animal we had seen since entering the woods, sat crouched upon the root of a tree a few feet from the water, apparently completely nonplused by the unexpected appearance of danger on the land side. All retreat was cut off, and he looked his fate in the face without flinching. I slaughtered him just as a savage would have done, and from the same motive, — I wanted his carcass to eat.

The mid-afternoon sun was now shining upon the lake, and a low, steady breeze drove the little waves rocking to the shore. A herd of cattle were browsing on the other side, and the bell of the leader sounded across the water. In these solitudes its clang was wild and musical.

To try the trout was the first thing in order. On a rude raft of logs which we found moored at the shore, and which with two aboard shipped about a foot of water, we floated out and wet our first fly in Thomas's Lake; but the trout refused to jump, and, to be frank, not more than a dozen and a half were caught during our stay. Only a week previous, a party of three had taken in a few hours all the fish they could carry out of the woods, and had nearly surfeited their neighbors with trout. But from some cause they now refused to rise, or to touch any kind of bait: so we fell to catching the sunfish, which were small but very abundant. Their nests were all along shore. A space about the size of a breakfast-plate was cleared of sediment and decayed vegetable matter, revealing the pebbly bottom, fresh and bright, with one or two fish suspended over the centre of it, keeping watch and ward. If an intruder approached, they would dart at him spitefully. These fish have the air of bantam cocks, and, with their sharp, prickly fins and spines and scaly sides, must be ugly customers in a hand-to-hand encounter with other finny warriors. To a hungry man they look about as unpromising as hemlock slivers, so thorny and thin are they; yet there is sweet meat in them, as we found that day.

Much refreshed, I set out with the sun low in the west to explore the outlet of the lake and try for trout there, while my companions made further trials in the lake itself. The outlet, as is usual in bodies of water of this kind, was very gentle and private. The stream, six or eight feet wide, flowed silently and evenly along for a distance of three or four rods, when it suddenly, as if conscious of its freedom, took a leap down some rocks. Thence, as far as I followed it, its descent was very rapid through a continuous succession of brief falls like so many steps down the mountain. Its appearance promised more trout than I found, though I returned to camp with a very respectable string.

Toward sunset I went round to explore the inlet, and found that as usual the stream wound leisurely through marshy ground. The water being much colder than in the outlet, the trout were more plentiful. As I was picking my way over the miry ground and through the rank growths, a ruffed grouse hopped up on a fallen branch a few paces before me, and, jerking his tail, threatened to take flight. But as I was at that moment gunless and remained stationary, he presently jumped down and walked away.

A seeker of birds, and ever on the alert for some new acquaintance, my attention was arrested, on first entering the swamp, by a bright, lively song, or warble, that issued from the branches overhead, and that was entirely new to me, though there was something in the tone of it that told me the bird was related to the wood-wagtail and to the water-wagtail or thrush. The strain was emphatic and quite loud, like the canary's, but very brief. The bird kept itself well secreted in the upper branches of the trees, and for a long time eluded my eye. I passed to and fro several times, and it seemed to break out afresh as I approached a certain little bend in the creek, and to cease after I had got beyond it; no doubt its nest was somewhere in the vicinity. After some delay the bird was sighted and brought down. It proved to be the small, or northern, water-thrush (called also the New York water-thrush), — a new bird to me. In size it was noticeably smaller than the large, or Louisiana, water-thrush, as described by Audubon, but in other respects its general appearance was the same. It was a great treat to me, and again I felt myself in luck.

This bird was unknown to the older ornithologists, and is but poorly described by the new. It builds a mossy nest on the ground, or under the edge of a decayed log. A correspondent writes me that he has found it breeding on the mountains in Pennsylvania. The large-billed water-thrush is much the superior songster, but the present species has a very bright and cheerful strain. The specimen I saw, contrary to the habits of the family, kept in the treetops like a warbler, and seemed to be engaged in catching insects.

The birds were unusually plentiful and noisy about the head of this lake; robins, blue jays, and woodpeckers greeted me with their familiar notes. The blue-jays found an owl or some wild animal a short distance above me, and, as is their custom on such occasions, proclaimed it at the top of their voices, and kept on till the darkness began to gather in the woods.

I also heard here, as I had at two or three other points in the course of the day, the peculiar, resonant hammering of some species of woodpecker upon the hard, dry limbs. It was unlike any sound of the kind I had ever before heard, and, repeated at intervals through the silent woods, was a very marked and characteristic feature. Its peculiarity was the ordered succession of the raps, which gave it the character of a premeditated performance. There were first three strokes following each other rapidly, then two much louder ones with longer intervals between them. I heard the drumming here, and the next day at sunset at Furlow Lake, the source of Dry Brook, and in no instance was the order varied. There was melody in it, such as a woodpecker knows how to evoke from a smooth, dry branch. It suggested something quite as pleasing as the liveliest bird-song, and was if anything more woodsy and wild. As the yellow-bellied woodpecker was the most abundant species in these woods, I attributed it to him. It is the one sound that still links itself with those scenes in my mind.

At sunset the grouse began to drum in all parts of the woods about the lake. I could hear five at one time, *thump, thump, thump, thump, thr-r-r-r-r-r-rr*. It was a homely, welcome sound. As I returned to camp at twilight, along the shore of the

lake, the frogs also were in full chorus. The older
ones ripped out their responses to each other with
terrific force and volume. I know of no other animal capable of giving forth so much sound, in proportion to its size, as a frog. Some of these seemed
to bellow as loud as a two-year-old bull. They
were of immense size, and very abundant. No
frog-eater had ever been there. Near the shore we
felled a tree which reached far out in the lake.
Upon the trunk and branches the frogs soon col-
lected in large numbers, and gamboled and splashed
about the half-submerged top, like a parcel of school-
boys, making nearly as much noise.

After dark, as I was frying the fish, a panful of
the largest trout was accidently capsized in the
fire. With rueful countenances we contemplated
the irreparable loss our commissariat had sustained
by this mishap; but remembering there was virtue
in ashes, we poked the half-consumed fish from the
bed of coals and ate them, and they were good.

We lodged that night on a brush-heap and slept
soundly. The green, yielding beech-twigs, covered
with a buffalo robe, were equal to a hair mattress.
The heat and smoke from a large fire kindled in the
afternoon had banished every "no-see-em" from
the locality, and in the morning the sun was above
the mountain before we awoke.

I immediately started again for the inlet, and
went far up the stream toward its source. A fair

string of trout for breakfast was my reward. The cattle with the bell were at the head of the valley, where they had passed the night. Most of them were two-year-old steers. They came up to me and begged for salt, and scared the fish by their importunities.

We finished our bread that morning, and ate every fish we could catch, and about ten o'clock prepared to leave the lake. The weather had been admirable, and the lake was a gem, and I would gladly have spent a week in the neighborhood; but the question of supplies was a serious one, and would brook no delay.

When we reached, on our return, the point where we had crossed the line of marked trees the day before, the question arose whether we should still trust ourselves to this line, or follow our own trail back to the spring and the battlement of rocks on the top of the mountain, and thence to the rock where the guide had left us. We decided in favor of the former course. After a march of three quarters of an hour the blazed trees ceased, and we concluded we were near the point at which we had parted with the guide. So we built a fire, laid down our loads, and cast about on all sides for some clew as to our exact locality. Nearly an hour was consumed in this manner, and without any result. I came upon a brood of young grouse, which diverted me for a moment. The old one blustered

about at a furious rate, trying to draw all attention
to herself, while the young ones, which were unable to fly, hid themselves. She whined like a dog
in great distress, and dragged herself along apparently with the greatest difficulty. As I pursued
her, she ran very nimbly, and presently flew a few
yards. Then, as I went on, she flew farther and
farther each time, till at last she got up, and went
humming through the woods as if she had no interest in them. I went back and caught one of the
young, which had simply squatted close to the
leaves. I took it up and set it on the palm of my
hand, which it hugged as closely as if still upon the
ground. I then put it in my coatsleeve, when it
ran and nestled in my armpit.

When we met at the sign of the smoke, opinions
differed as to the most feasible course. There was
no doubt but that we could get out of the woods;
but we wished to get out speedily, and as near as
possible to the point where we had entered. Half
ashamed of our timidity and indecision, we finally
tramped away back to where we had crossed the line
of blazed trees, followed our old trail to the spring
on the top of the range, and, after much searching
and scouring to the right and left, found ourselves
at the very place we had left two hours before.
Another deliberation and a divided council. But
something must be done. It was then mid-afternoon, and the prospect of spending another night

on the mountains, without food or drink, was not pleasant. So we moved down the ridge. Here another line of marked trees was found, the course of which formed an obtuse angle with the one we had followed. It kept on the top of the ridge for perhaps a mile, when it entirely disappeared, and we were as much adrift as ever. Then one of the party swore an oath, and said he was going out of those woods, hit or miss, and, wheeling to the right, instantly plunged over the brink of the mountain. The rest followed, but would fain have paused and ciphered away at their own uncertainties, to see if a certainty could not be arrived at as to where we would come out. But our bold leader was solving the problem in the right way. Down and down and still down we went, as if we were to bring up in the bowels of the earth. It was by far the steepest descent we had made, and we felt a grim satisfaction in knowing that we could not retrace our steps this time, be the issue what it might. As we paused on the brink of a ledge of rocks, we chanced to see through the trees distant cleared land. A house or barn also was dimly descried. This was encouraging ; but we could not make out whether it was on Beaver Kill or Mill Brook or Dry Brook, and did not long stop to consider where it was. We at last brought up at the bottom of a deep gorge, through which flowed a rapid creek that literally swarmed with trout. But we were in no

mood to catch them, and pushed on along the channel of the stream, sometimes leaping from rock to
rock, and sometimes splashing heedlessly through
the water, and speculating the while as to where
we should probably come out. On the Beaver Kill,
my companions thought; but, from the position of
the sun, I said, on the Mill Brook, about six miles
below our team; for I remembered having seen, in
coming up this stream, a deep, wild valley that led
up into the mountains, like this one. Soon the
banks of the stream became lower, and we moved
into the woods. Here we entered upon an obscure
wood-road, which presently conducted us into the
midst of a vast hemlock forest. The land had a
gentle slope, and we wondered why the lumbermen
and barkmen who prowl through these woods had
left this fine tract untouched. Beyond this the
forest was mostly birch and maple.

We were now close to the settlement, and began
to hear human sounds. One rod more, and we
were out of the woods. It took us a moment to
comprehend the scene. Things looked very strange
at first; but quickly they began to change and to
put on familiar features. Some magic scene-shift-
ing seemed to take place before my eyes, till, instead of the unknown settlement which I at first
seemed to look upon, there stood the farmhouse at
which we had stopped two days before, and at the
same moment we heard the stamping of our team in

the barn. We sat down and laughed heartily over our good luck. Our desperate venture had resulted better than we had dared to hope, and had shamed our wisest plans. At the house our arrival had been anticipated about this time, and dinner was being put upon the table.

It was then five o'clock, so that we had been in the woods just forty-eight hours; but if time is only phenomenal, as the philosophers say, and life only in feeling, as the poets aver, we were some months, if not years, older at that moment than we had been two days before. Yet younger, too, — though this be a paradox, — for the birches had infused into us some of their own suppleness and strength.

1869.

Woodchuck Lodge, front entrance. Drawing by Jean Fader.

THE SNOW-WALKERS

HE who marvels at the beauty of the world in summer will find equal cause for wonder and admiration in winter. It is true the pomp and the pageantry are swept away, but the essential elements remain, — the day and the night, the mountain and the valley, the elemental play and succession and the perpetual presence of the infinite sky. In winter the stars seem to have rekindled their fires, the moon achieves a fuller triumph, and the heavens wear a look of a more exalted simplicity. Summer is more wooing and seductive, more versatile and human, appeals to the affections and the sentiments, and fosters inquiry and the art impulse. Winter is of a more heroic cast, and addresses the intellect. The severe studies and disciplines come easier in winter. One imposes larger tasks upon himself, and is less tolerant of his own weaknesses.

The tendinous part of the mind, so to speak, is more developed in winter; the fleshy, in summer. I should say winter had given the bone and sinew to Literature, summer the tissues and blood.

The simplicity of winter has a deep moral. The

return of nature, after such a career of splendor and prodigality, to habits so simple and austere, is not lost upon either the head or the heart. It is the philosopher coming back from the banquet and the wine to a cup of water and a crust of bread.

And then this beautiful masquerade of the elements, — the novel disguises our nearest friends put on! Here is another rain and another dew, water that will not flow, nor spill, nor receive the taint of an unclean vessel. And if we see truly, the same old beneficence and willingness to serve lurk beneath all.

Look up at the miracle of the falling snow, — the air a dizzy maze of whirling, eddying flakes, noiselessly transforming the world, the exquisite crystals dropping in ditch and gutter, and disguising in the same suit of spotless livery all objects upon which they fall. How novel and fine the first drifts! The old, dilapidated fence is suddenly set off with the most fantastic ruffles, scalloped and fluted after an unheard-of fashion! Looking down a long line of decrepit stone wall, in the trimming of which the wind had fairly run riot, I saw, as for the first time, what a severe yet master artist old Winter is. Ah, a severe artist! How stern the woods look, dark and cold and as rigid against the horizon as iron!

All life and action upon the snow have an added emphasis and significance. Every expression is underscored. Summer has few finer pictures than

this winter one of the farmer foddering his cattle
from a stack upon the clean snow, — the movement,
the sharply defined figures, the great green flakes of
hay, the long file of patient cows, the advance just
arriving and pressing eagerly for the choicest morsels, — and the bounty and providence it suggests.
Or the chopper in the woods, — the prostrate tree,
the white new chips scattered about, his easy triumph over the cold, his coat hanging to a limb, and
the clear, sharp ring of his axe. The woods are
rigid and tense, keyed up by the frost, and resound
like a stringed instrument. Or the road-breakers,
sallying forth with oxen and sleds in the still, white
world, the day after the storm, to restore the lost
track and demolish the beleaguering drifts.

All sounds are sharper in winter; the air transmits better. At night I hear more distinctly the
steady roar of the North Mountain. In summer it
is a sort of complacent purr, as the breezes stroke
down its sides; but in winter always the same low,
sullen growl.

A severe artist! No longer the canvas and the
pigments, but the marble and the chisel. When
the nights are calm and the moon full, I go out to
gaze upon the wonderful purity of the moonlight
and the snow. The air is full of latent fire, and
the cold warms me — after a different fashion from
that of the kitchen stove. The world lies about me
in a "trance of snow." The clouds are pearly and

iridescent, and seem the farthest possible remove from the condition of a storm, — the ghosts of clouds, the indwelling beauty freed from all dross. I see the hills, bulging with great drifts, lift themselves up cold and white against the sky, the black lines of fences here and there obliterated by the depth of the snow. Presently a fox barks away up next the mountain, and I imagine I can almost see him sitting there, in his furs, upon the illuminated surface, and looking down in my direction. As I listen, one answers him from behind the woods in the valley. What a wild winter sound, wild and weird, up among the ghostly hills! Since the wolf has ceased to howl upon these mountains, and the panther to scream, there is nothing to be compared with it. So wild! I get up in the middle of the night to hear it. It is refreshing to the ear, and one delights to know that such wild creatures are among us. At this season Nature makes the most of every throb of life that can withstand her severity. How heartily she indorses this fox! In what bold relief stand out the lives of all walkers of the snow! The snow is a great tell-tale, and blabs as effectually as it obliterates. I go into the woods, and know all that has happened. I cross the fields, and if only a mouse has visited his neighbor, the fact is chronicled.

The red fox is the only species that abounds in my locality; the little gray fox seems to prefer a more rocky and precipitous country, and a less rigorous climate; the cross fox is occasionally seen, and there are traditions of the silver gray among the oldest hunters. But the red fox is the sportsman's prize, and the only fur-bearer worthy of note in these mountains.[1] I go out in the morning, after a fresh fall of snow, and see at all points where he has crossed the road. Here he has leisurely passed within rifle-range of the house, evidently reconnoitring the premises with an eye to the hen-roost. That clear, sharp track, — there is no mistaking it for the clumsy footprint of a little dog. All his wildness and agility are photographed in it. Here he has taken fright, or suddenly recollected an engagement, and in long, graceful leaps, barely touching the fence, has gone careering up the hill as fleet as the wind.

The wild, buoyant creature, how beautiful he is! I had often seen his dead carcass, and at a distance had witnessed the hounds drive him across the upper fields; but the thrill and excitement of meeting him in his wild freedom in the woods were unknown to me till, one cold winter day, drawn thither by the baying of a hound, I stood near the summit of the mountain, waiting a renewal of the sound, that I might determine the course of the dog and choose my position, — stimulated by the ambition of all young Nimrods to bag some notable game. Long

[1] A spur of the Catskills.

I waited, and patiently, till, chilled and benumbed, I was about to turn back, when, hearing a slight noise, I looked up and beheld a most superb fox, loping along with inimitable grace and ease, evidently disturbed, but not pursued by the hound, and so absorbed in his private meditations that he failed to see me, though I stood transfixed with amazement and admiration, not ten yards distant. I took his measure at a glance, — a large male, with dark legs, and massive tail tipped with white, — a most magnificent creature; but so astonished and fascinated was I by this sudden appearance and matchless beauty, that not till I had caught the last glimpse of him, as he disappeared over a knoll, did I awake to my duty as a sportsman, and realize what an opportunity to distinguish myself I had unconsciously let slip. I clutched my gun, half angrily, as if it was to blame, and went home out of humor with myself and all fox-kind. But I have since thought better of the experience, and concluded that I bagged the game after all, the best part of it, and fleeced Reynard of something more valuable than his fur, without his knowledge.

This is thoroughly a winter sound, — this voice of the hound upon the mountain, — and one that is music to many ears. The long trumpet-like bay, heard for a mile or more, — now faintly back in the deep recesses of the mountain, — now distinct, but still faint, as the hound comes over some prominent

point and the wind favors, — anon entirely lost in
the gully, — then breaking out again much nearer,
and growing more and more pronounced as the dog
approaches, till, when he comes around the brow
of the mountain, directly above you, the barking
is loud and sharp. On he goes along the northern spur, his voice rising and sinking as the wind
and the lay of the ground modify it, till lost to
hearing.

The fox usually keeps half a mile ahead, regulat-
ing his speed by that of the hound, occasionally
pausing a moment to divert himself with a mouse,
or to contemplate the landscape, or to listen for his
pursuer. If the hound press him too closely, he
leads off from mountain to mountain, and so generally escapes the hunter ; but if the pursuit be
slow, he plays about some ridge or peak, and falls
a prey, though not an easy one, to the experienced
sportsman.

A most spirited and exciting chase occurs when the
farm-dog gets close upon one in the open field, as
sometimes happens in the early morning. The fox
relies so confidently upon his superior speed, that I
imagine he half tempts the dog to the race. But if
the dog be a smart one, and their course lie downhill, over smooth ground, Reynard must put his
best foot forward, and then sometimes suffer the
ignominy of being run over by his pursuer, who,
however, is quite unable to pick him up, owing to

the speed. But when they mount the hill, or enter
the woods, the superior nimbleness and agility of the
fox tell at once, and he easily leaves the dog far in
his rear. For a cur less than his own size he mani-
fests little fear, especially if the two meet alone,
remote from the house. In such cases, I have seen
first one turn tail, then the other.

A novel spectacle often occurs in summer, when
the female has young. You are rambling on the
mountain, accompanied by your dog, when you are
startled by that wild, half-threatening squall, and
in a moment perceive your dog, with inverted tail,
and shame and confusion in his looks, sneaking
toward you, the old fox but a few rods in his rear.
You speak to him sharply, when he bristles up,
turns about, and, barking, starts off vigorously, as
if to wipe out the dishonor; but in a moment comes
sneaking back more abashed than ever, and owns
himself unworthy to be called a dog. The fox fairly
shames him out of the woods. The secret of the
matter is her sex, though her conduct, for the honor
of the fox be it said, seems to be prompted only by
solicitude for the safety of her young.

One of the most notable features of the fox is his
large and massive tail. Seen running on the snow
at a distance, his tail is quite as conspicuous as his
body; and, so far from appearing a burden, seems
to contribute to his lightness and buoyancy. It
softens the outline of his movements, and repeats or

continues to the eye the ease and poise of his carriage. But, pursued by the hound on a wet, thawy
day, it often becomes so heavy and bedraggled as to
prove a serious inconvenience, and compels him to
take refuge in his den. He is very loath to do this;
both his pride and the traditions of his race stimu-
late him to run it out, and win by fair superiority
of wind and speed ; and only a wound or a heavy
and moppish tail will drive him to avoid the issue
in this manner.

To learn his surpassing shrewdness and cunning,
attempt to take him with a trap. Rogue that he
is, he always suspects some trick, and one must be
more of a fox than he is himself to overreach him.
At first sight it would appear easy enough. With
apparent indifference he crosses your path, or walks
in your footsteps in the field, or travels along the
beaten highway, or lingers in the vicinity of stacks
and remote barns. Carry the carcass of a pig,
or a fowl, or a dog, to a distant field in midwinter, and in a few nights his tracks cover the snow
about it.

The inexperienced country youth, misled by this
seeming carelessness of Reynard, suddenly conceives
a project to enrich himself with fur, and wonders
that the idea has not occurred to him before, and
to others. I knew a youthful yeoman of this kind,
who imagined he had found a mine of wealth on
discovering on a remote side-hill, between two woods,

a dead porker, upon which it appeared all the foxes
of the neighborhood had nightly banqueted. The
clouds were burdened with snow; and as the first
flakes commenced to eddy down, he set out, trap
and broom in hand, already counting over in imagination the silver quarters he would receive for his
first fox-skin. With the utmost care, and with a
palpitating heart, he removed enough of the trodden
snow to allow the trap to sink below the surface.
Then, carefully sifting the light element over it
and sweeping his tracks full, he quickly withdrew,
laughing exultingly over the little surprise he had
prepared for the cunning rogue. The elements con-
spired to aid him, and the falling snow rapidly obliterated all vestiges of his work. The next morning
at dawn he was on his way to bring in his fur.
The snow had done its work effectually, and, he
believed, had kept his secret well. Arrived in sight
of the locality, he strained his vision to make out
his prize lodged against the fence at the foot of the
hill. Approaching nearer, the surface was unbroken,
and doubt usurped the place of certainty in his
mind. A slight mound marked the site of the
porker, but there was no footprint near it. Looking up the hill, he saw where Reynard had walked
leisurely down toward his wonted bacon till within
a few yards of it, when he had wheeled, and with
prodigious strides disappeared in the woods. The
young trapper saw at a glance what a comment this

was upon his skill in the art, and, indignantly exhuming the iron, he walked home with it, the stream of silver quarters suddenly setting in another direction.

The successful trapper commences in the fall, or before the first deep snow. In a field not too remote, with an old axe he cuts a small place, say ten inches by fourteen, in the frozen ground, and removes the earth to the depth of three or four inches, then fills the cavity with dry ashes, in which are placed bits of roasted cheese. Reynard is very suspicious at first, and gives the place a wide berth. It looks like design, and he will see how the thing behaves before he approaches too near. But the cheese is savory and the cold severe. He ventures a little closer every night, until he can reach and pick a piece from the surface. Emboldened by success, like other mortals, he presently digs freely among the ashes, and, finding a fresh supply of the delectable morsels every night, is soon thrown off his guard and his suspicions quite lulled. After a week of baiting in this manner, and on the eve of a light fall of snow, the trapper carefully conceals his trap in the bed, first smoking it thoroughly with hemlock boughs to kill or neutralize the smell of the iron. If the weather favors and the proper precautions have been taken, he may succeed, though the chances are still greatly against him.

Reynard is usually caught very lightly, seldom

more than the ends of his toes being between the
jaws.   He sometimes works so cautiously as to
spring the trap without injury even to his toes, or
may remove the cheese night after night without
even springing it. I knew an old trapper who, on
finding himself outwitted in this manner, tied a bit
of cheese to the pan, and next morning had poor
Reynard by the jaw. The trap is not fastened, but
only encumbered with a clog, and is all the more
sure in its hold by yielding to every effort of the
animal to extricate himself.

When Reynard sees his captor approaching, he
would fain drop into a mouse-hole to render himself
invisible. He crouches to the ground and remains
perfectly motionless until he perceives himself discovered, when he makes one desperate and final
effort to escape, but ceases all struggling as you
come up, and behaves in a manner that stamps him
a very timid warrior, — cowering to the earth with
a mingled look of shame, guilt, and abject fear. A
young farmer told me of tracing one with his trap
to the border of a wood, where he discovered the
cunning rogue trying to hide by embracing a small
tree. Most animals, when taken in a trap, show
fight; but Reynard has more faith in the nimbleness of his feet than in the terror of his teeth.

Entering the woods, the number and variety of
the tracks contrast strongly with the rigid, frozen
aspect of things. Warm jets of life still shoot and

play amid this snowy desolation. Fox-tracks are far less numerous than in the fields; but those of hares, skunks, partridges, squirrels, and mice abound. The mice tracks are very pretty, and look like a sort of fantastic stitching on the coverlid of the snow. One is curious to know what brings these tiny creatures from their retreats; they do not seem to be in quest of food, but rather to be traveling about for pleasure or sociability, though always going post-haste, and linking stump with stump and tree with tree by fine, hurried strides. That is when they travel openly; but they have hidden passages and winding galleries under the snow, which undoubtedly are their main avenues of communication. Here and there these passages rise so near the surface as to be covered by only a frail arch of snow, and a slight ridge betrays their course to the eye. I know him well. He is known to the farmer as the " deer mouse," to the naturalist as the white-footed mouse, — a very beautiful creature, nocturnal in his habits, with large ears, and large, fine eyes full of a wild, harmless look. He is daintily marked, with white feet and a white belly. When disturbed by day he is very easily captured, having none of the cunning or viciousness of the common Old World mouse.

It is he who, high in the hollow trunk of some tree, lays by a store of beechnuts for winter use. Every nut is carefully shelled, and the cavity that

serves as storehouse lined with grass and leaves.
The wood-chopper frequently squanders this precious store. I have seen half a peck taken from one
tree, as clean and white as if put up by the most
delicate hands, — as they were. How long it must
have taken the little creature to collect this quan-
tity, to hull them one by one, and convey them up
to his fifth-story chamber! He is not confined to
the woods, but is quite as common in the fields,
particularly in the fall, amid the corn and potatoes.
When routed by the plow, I have seen the old
one take flight with half a dozen young hanging to
her teats, and with such reckless speed that some
of the young would lose their hold and fly off amid
the weeds. Taking refuge in a stump with the rest
of her family, the anxious mother would presently
come back and hunt up the missing ones.

The snow-walkers are mostly night-walkers also,
and the record they leave upon the snow is the main
clew one has to their life and doings. The hare
is nocturnal in its habits, and though a very lively
creature at night, with regular courses and run-ways
through the wood, is entirely quiet by day. Timid
as he is, he makes little effort to conceal himself,
usually squatting beside a log, stump, or tree, and
seeming to avoid rocks and ledges, where he might
be partially housed from the cold and the snow,
but where also — and this consideration undoubtedly determines his choice — he would be more apt

to fall a prey to his enemies. In this, as well as
in many other respects, he differs from the rabbit
proper: he never burrows in the ground, or takes
refuge in a den or hole, when pursued. If caught
in the open fields, he is much confused and easily
overtaken by the dog; but in the woods, he leaves
him at a bound. In summer, when first disturbed,
he beats the ground violently with his feet, by
which means he would express to you his surprise
or displeasure; it is a dumb way he has of scolding.
After leaping a few yards, he pauses an instant,
as if to determine the degree of danger, and then
hurries away with a much lighter tread.

His feet are like great pads, and his track has
little of the sharp, articulated expression of Reynard's, or of animals that climb or dig. Yet it is
very pretty like all the rest, and tells its own tale.
There is nothing bold or vicious or vulpine in it,
and his timid, harmless character is published at
every leap. He abounds in dense woods, preferring
localities filled with a small undergrowth of beech
and birch, upon the bark of which he feeds. Nature
is rather partial to him, and matches his extreme
local habits and character with a suit that corresponds with his surroundings, — reddish gray in
summer and white in winter.

The sharp-rayed track of the partridge adds another figure to this fantastic embroidery upon the
winter snow. Her course is a clear, strong line,

sometimes quite wayward, but generally very direct, steering for the densest, most impenetrable places, — leading you over logs and through brush, alert and expectant, till, suddenly, she bursts up a few yards from you, and goes humming through the trees, — the complete triumph of endurance and vigor. Hardy native bird, may your tracks never be fewer, or your visits to the birch-tree less frequent!

The squirrel tracks — sharp, nervous, and wiry — have their histories also. But how rarely we see squirrels in winter! The naturalists say they are mostly torpid; yet evidently that little pocket-faced depredator, the chipmunk, was not carrying buckwheat for so many days to his hole for nothing: was he anticipating a state of torpidity, or providing against the demands of a very active appetite? Red and gray squirrels are more or less active all winter, though very shy, and, I am inclined to think, partially nocturnal in their habits. Here a gray one has just passed, — came down that tree and went up this; there he dug for a beechnut, and left the burr on the snow. How did he know where to dig? During an unusually severe winter I have known him to make long journeys to a barn, in a remote field, where wheat was stored. How did he know there was wheat there? In attempting to return, the adventurous creature was frequently run down and caught in the deep snow.

His home is in the trunk of some old birch or maple, with an entrance far up amid the branches. In the spring he builds himself a summer-house of small leafy twigs in the top of a neighboring beech, where the young are reared and much of the time is passed. But the safer retreat in the maple is not abandoned, and both old and young resort thither in the fall, or when danger threatens. Whether this temporary residence amid the branches is for elegance or pleasure, or for sanitary reasons or domestic convenience, the naturalist has forgotten to mention.

The elegant creature, so cleanly in its habits, so graceful in its carriage, so nimble and daring in its movements, excites feelings of admiration akin to those awakened by the birds and the fairer forms of nature. His passage through the trees is almost a flight. Indeed, the flying squirrel has little or no advantage over him, and in speed and nimbleness cannot compare with him at all. If he miss his footing and fall, he is sure to catch on the next branch; if the connection be broken, he leaps recklessly for the nearest spray or limb, and secures his hold, even if it be by the aid of his teeth.

His career of frolic and festivity begins in the fall, after the birds have left us and the holiday spirit of nature has commenced to subside. How absorbing the pastime of the sportsman who goes to the woods in the still October morning in quest of him! You step lightly across the threshold of the forest, and sit down upon the first log or rock to await the signals. It is so still that the ear suddenly seems to have acquired new powers, and there is no movement to confuse the eye. Presently you hear the rustling of a branch, and see it sway or spring as the squirrel leaps from or to it; or else you hear a disturbance in the dry leaves, and mark one running upon the ground. He has probably seen the intruder, and, not liking his stealthy movements, desires to avoid a nearer acquaintance. Now he mounts a stump to see if the way is clear, then pauses a moment at the foot of a tree to take his bearings, his tail, as he skims along, undulating behind him, and adding to the easy grace and dignity of his movements. Or else you are first advised of his proximity by the dropping of a false nut, or the fragments of the shucks rattling upon the leaves. Or, again, after contemplating you awhile unobserved, and making up his mind that you are not dangerous, he strikes an attitude on a branch, and commences to quack and bark, with an accompanying movement of his tail. Late in the afternoon, when the same stillness reigns, the same scenes are repeated. There is a black variety, quite rare, but mating freely with the gray, from which he seems to be distinguished only in color.

The track of the red squirrel may be known by its smaller size. He is more common and less dig-

nified than the gray, and oftener guilty of petty lar-
ceny about the barns and grain-fields. He is most
abundant in old barkpeelings, and low, dilapidated
hemlocks, from which he makes excursions to the
fields and orchards, spinning along the tops of the
fences, which afford not only convenient lines of
communication, but a safe retreat if danger threatens. He loves to linger about the orchard; and,
sitting upright on the topmost stone in the wall, or
on the tallest stake in the fence, chipping up an
apple for the seeds, his tail conforming to the curve
of his back, his paws shifting and turning the apple,
he is a pretty sight, and his bright, pert appearance
atones for all the mischief he does. At home, in
the woods, he is the most frolicsome and loquacious.
The appearance of anything unusual, if, after contemplating it a moment, he concludes it not dangerous, excites his unbounded mirth and ridicule,
and he snickers and chatters, hardly able to contain
himself; now darting up the trunk of a tree and
squealing in derision, then hopping into position
on a limb and dancing to the music of his own
cackle, and all for your special benefit.

There is something very human in this apparent
mirth and mockery of the squirrels. It seems to
be a sort of ironical laughter, and implies self-conscious pride and exultation in the laugher. "What
a ridiculous thing you are, to be sure!" he seems to
say; "how clumsy and awkward, and what a poor

show for a tail! Look at me, look at me!" — and
he capers about in his best style. Again, he would
seem to tease you and provoke your attention; then
suddenly assumes a tone of good-natured, childlike
defiance and derision. That pretty little imp, the
chipmunk, will sit on the stone above his den and
defy you, as plainly as if he said so, to catch him
before he can get into his hole if you can. You
hurl a stone at him, and "No you did n't!" comes
up from the depth of his retreat.

In February another track appears upon the
snow, slender and delicate, about a third larger than
that of the gray squirrel, indicating no haste or
speed, but, on the contrary, denoting the most im-
perturbable ease and leisure, the footprints so close
together that the trail appears like a chain of curiously carved links. Sir *Mephitis mephitica*, or,
in plain English, the skunk, has awakened from his
six weeks' nap, and come out into society again.
He is a nocturnal traveler, very bold and impudent,
coming quite up to the barn and outbuildings, and
sometimes taking up his quarters for the season
under the haymow. There is no such word as hurry
in his dictionary, as you may see by his path upon
the snow. He has a very sneaking, insinuating
way, and goes creeping about the fields and woods,
never once in a perceptible degree altering his gait,
and, if a fence crosses his course, steers for a break
or opening to avoid climbing. He is too indolent

even to dig his own hole, but appropriates that of
a woodchuck, or hunts out a crevice in the rocks,
from which he extends his rambling in all directions, preferring damp, thawy weather. He has
very little discretion or cunning, and holds a trap
in utter contempt, stepping into it as soon as beside it, relying implicitly for defense against all
forms of danger upon the unsavory punishment he
is capable of inflicting. He is quite indifferent to
both man and beast, and will not hurry himself to
get out of the way of either. Walking through the
summer fields at twilight, I have come near stepping upon him, and was much the more disturbed
of the two. When attacked in the open field he
confounds the plans of his enemies by the unheard-
of tactics of exposing his rear rather than his front.
"Come if you dare," he says, and his attitude
makes even the farm-dog pause. After a few en-
counters of this kind, and if you entertain the usual
hostility towards him, your mode of attack will
speedily resolve itself into moving about him in a
circle, the radius of which will be the exact distance
at which you can hurl a stone with accuracy and
effect.

He has a secret to keep and knows it, and is
careful not to betray himself until he can do so with
the most telling effect. I have known him to preserve his serenity even when caught in a steel trap,
and look the very picture of injured innocence,

manœuvring carefully and deliberately to extricate his foot from the grasp of the naughty jaws. Do not by any means take pity on him, and lend a helping hand!

How pretty his face and head! How fine and delicate his teeth, like a weasel's or a cat's! When about a third grown, he looks so well that one covets him for a pet. He is quite precocious, however, and capable, even at this tender age, of making a very strong appeal to your sense of smell.

No animal is more cleanly in his habits than he. He is not an awkward boy who cuts his own face with his whip; and neither his flesh nor his fur hints the weapon with which he is armed. The most silent creature known to me, he makes no sound, so far as I have observed, save a diffuse, impatient noise, like that produced by beating your hand with a whisk-broom, when the farm-dog has discovered his retreat in the stone fence. He renders himself obnoxious to the farmer by his partiality for hens' eggs and young poultry. He is a confirmed epicure, and at plundering hen-roosts an expert. Not the full-grown fowls are his victims, but the youngest and most tender. At night Mother Hen receives under her maternal wings a dozen newly hatched chickens, and with much pride and satisfaction feels them all safely tucked away in her feathers. In the morning she is walking about disconsolately, attended by only two or three of all

that pretty brood. What has happened? Where
are they gone? That pickpocket, Sir Mephitis,
could solve the mystery. Quietly has he approached,
under cover of darkness, and one by one relieved
her of her precious charge. Look closely and you
will see their little yellow legs and beaks, or part
of a mangled form, lying about on the ground. Or,
before the hen has hatched, he may find her out,
and, by the same sleight of hand, remove every egg,
leaving only the empty blood-stained shells to wit-
ness against him. The birds, especially the ground-
builders, suffer in like manner from his plundering
propensities.

The secretion upon which he relies for defense,
and which is the chief source of his unpopularity,
while it affords good reasons against cultivating him
as a pet, and mars his attractiveness as game, is by
no means the greatest indignity that can be offered
to a nose. It is a rank, living smell, and has none
of the sickening qualities of disease or putrefaction.
Indeed, I think a good smeller will enjoy its most
refined intensity. It approaches the sublime, and
makes the nose tingle. It is tonic and bracing, and,
I can readily believe, has rare medicinal qualities.
I do not recommend its use as eyewater, though an
old farmer assures me it has undoubted virtues when
thus applied. Hearing, one night, a disturbance
among his hens, he rushed suddenly out to catch
the thief, when Sir Mephitis, taken by surprise, and

no doubt much annoyed at being interrupted, discharged the vials of his wrath full in the farmer's
face, and with such admirable effect that, for a few
moments, he was completely blinded, and powerless
to revenge himself upon the rogue, who embraced
the opportunity to make good his escape; but he
declared that afterwards his eyes felt as if purged
by fire, and his sight was much clearer.

In March that brief summary of a bear, the raccoon, comes out of his den in the ledges, and leaves
his sharp digitigrade track upon the snow, — traveling not unfrequently in pairs, — a lean, hungry
couple, bent on pillage and plunder. They have
an unenviable time of it, — feasting in the summer
and fall, hibernating in winter, and starving in
spring. In April I have found the young of the
previous year creeping about the fields, so reduced
by starvation as to be quite helpless, and offering
no resistance to my taking them up by the tail and
carrying them home.

The old ones also become very much emaciated,
and come boldly up to the barn or other outbuildings in quest of food. I remember, one morning in
early spring, of hearing old Cuff, the farm-dog, barking vociferously before it was yet light. When we
got up we discovered him, at the foot of an ash-tree
standing about thirty rods from the house, looking
up at some gray object in the leafless branches, and
by his manners and his voice evincing great impa-

tience that we were so tardy in coming to his assistance. Arrived on the spot, we saw in the tree a coon of unusual size. One bold climber proposed to go up and shake him down. This was what old Cuff wanted, and he fairly bounded with delight as he saw his young master shinning up the tree. Approaching within eight or ten feet of the coon, he seized the branch to which it clung and shook long and fiercely. But the coon was in no danger of losing its hold, and, when the climber paused to renew his hold, it turned toward him with a growl, and showed very clearly a purpose to advance to the attack. This caused his pursuer to descend to the ground with all speed. When the coon was finally brought down with a gun, he fought the dog, which was a large, powerful animal, with great fury, returning bite for bite for some moments; and after a quarter of an hour had elapsed and his unequal antagonist had shaken him as a terrier does a rat, making his teeth meet through the small of his back, the coon still showed fight.

They are very tenacious of life, and like the badger will always whip a dog of their own size and weight. A woodchuck can bite severely, having teeth that cut like chisels, but a coon has agility and power of limb as well.

They are considered game only in the fall, or towards the close of summer, when they become fat and their flesh sweet. At this time, cooning in the

remote interior is a famous pastime. As this animal
is entirely nocturnal in its habits, it is hunted only
at night. A piece of corn on some remote side-hill
near the mountain, or between two pieces of woods,
is most apt to be frequented by them. While the
corn is yet green they pull the ears down like hogs,
and, tearing open the sheathing of husks, eat the
tender, succulent kernels, bruising and destroying
much more than they devour. Sometimes their
ravages are a matter of serious concern to the farmer.
But every such neighborhood has its coon-dog, and
the boys and young men dearly love the sport.
The party sets out about eight or nine o'clock of a
dark, moonless night, and stealthily approaches the
cornfield. The dog knows his business, and when
he is put into a patch of corn and told to "hunt them
up" he makes a thorough search, and will not be
misled by any other scent. You hear him rattling
through the corn, hither and yon, with great speed.
The coons prick up their ears, and leave on the
opposite side of the field. In the stillness you may
sometimes hear a single stone rattle on the wall as
they hurry toward the woods. If the dog finds
nothing, he comes back to his master in a short time,
and says in his dumb way, "No coon there." But
if he strikes a trail, you presently hear a louder rattling on the stone wall, and then a hurried bark as
he enters the woods, followed in a few minutes by
loud and repeated barking as he reaches the foot of

the tree in which the coon has taken refuge. Then follows a pellmell rush of the cooning party up the hill, into the woods, through the brush and the darkness, falling over prostrate trees, pitching into gullies and hollows, losing hats and tearing clothes, till finally, guided by the baying of the faithful dog, the tree is reached. The first thing now in order is to kindle a fire, and, if its light reveals the coon, to shoot him; if not, to fell the tree with an axe. If this happens to be too great a sacrifice of timber and of strength, to sit down at the foot of the tree till morning.

But with March our interest in these phases of animal life, which winter has so emphasized and brought out, begins to decline. Vague rumors are afloat in the air of a great and coming change. We are eager for Winter to be gone, since he, too, is fugitive and cannot keep his place. Invisible hands deface his icy statuary; his chisel has lost its cunning. The drifts, so pure and exquisite, are now earth-stained and weather-worn, — the flutes and scallops, and fine, firm lines, all gone; and what was a grace and an ornament to the hills is now a disfiguration. Like worn and unwashed linen appear the remains of that spotless robe with which he clothed the world as his bride.

But he will not abdicate without a struggle. Day after day he rallies his scattered forces, and night after night pitches his white tents on the hills, and would fain regain his lost ground; but the young prince in every encounter prevails. Slowly and reluctantly the gray old hero retreats up the mountain, till finally the south rain comes in earnest, and in a night he is dead.

Catskills, view from the front porch of Woodchuck Lodge.
Drawing by Jean Fader.

AUTUMN TIDES

THE season is always a little behind the sun in our climate, just as the tide is always a little behind the moon. According to the calendar, the summer ought to culminate about the 21st of June, but in reality it is some weeks later; June is a maiden month all through. It is not high noon in nature till about the first or second week in July. When the chestnut-tree blooms, the meridian of the year is reached. By the first of August it is fairly one o'clock. The lustre of the season begins to dim, the foliage of the trees and woods to tarnish, the plumage of the birds to fade, and their songs to cease. The hints of approaching fall are on every hand. How suggestive this thistle-down, for instance, which, as I sit by the open window, comes in and brushes softly across my hand! The first snowflake tells of winter not more plainly than this driving down heralds the approach of fall. Come here, my fairy, and tell me whence you come and whither you go? What brings you to port here, you gossamer ship sailing the great sea? How exquisitely frail and delicate! One of the lightest things in nature; so light that in the closed room here it will hardly rest in my open palm. A feather is a clod beside it. Only a spider's web will hold it; coarser objects have no power over it. Caught in the upper currents of the air and rising above the clouds, it might sail perpetually. Indeed, one fancies it might almost traverse the interstellar ether and drive against the stars. And every thistle-head by the roadside holds hundreds of these sky rovers, — imprisoned Ariels unable to set themselves free. Their liberation may be by the shock of the wind, or the rude contact of cattle, but it is oftener the work of the goldfinch with its complaining brood. The seed of the thistle is the proper food of this bird, and in obtaining it myriads of these winged creatures are scattered to the breeze. Each one is fraught with a seed which it exists to sow, but its wild careering and soaring does not fairly begin till its burden is dropped, and its spheral form is complete. The seeds of many plants and trees are disseminated through the agency of birds; but the thistle furnishes its own birds, — flocks of them, with wings more ethereal and tireless than were ever given to mortal creature. From the pains Nature thus takes to sow the thistle broadcast over the land, it might be expected to be one of the most troublesome and abundant of weeds. But such is not the case; the more pernicious and baffling weeds, like snapdragon or blind nettles, are more local and restricted in their habits, and unable to fly at all.

In the fall, the battles of the spring are fought over again, beginning at the other or little end of the series. There is the same advance and retreat, with many feints and alarms, between the contending forces, that was witnessed in April and May. The spring comes like a tide running against a strong wind; it is ever beaten back, but ever gaining ground, with now and then a mad "push upon the land" as if to overcome its antagonist at one blow. The cold from the north encroaches upon us in about the same fashion. In September or early in October it usually makes a big stride forward and blackens all the more delicate plants, and hastens the "mortal ripening" of the foliage of the trees, but it is presently beaten back again, and the genial warmth repossesses the land. Before long, however, the cold returns to the charge with augmented forces and gains much ground.

The course of the seasons never does run smooth, owing to the unequal distribution of land and water, mountain, wood, and plain.

An equilibrium, however, is usually reached in our climate in October, sometimes the most marked in November, forming the delicious Indian summer; a truce is declared, and both forces, heat and cold, meet and mingle in friendly converse on the field. In the earlier season, this poise of the temperature,

this slack-water in nature, comes in May and June;
but the October calm is most marked. Day after
day, and sometimes week after week, you cannot tell
which way the current is setting. Indeed, there is
no current, but the season seems to drift a little this
way or a little that, just as the breeze happens to
freshen a little in one quarter or the other. The fall
of '74 was the most remarkable in this respect I
remember ever to have seen. The equilibrium of
the season lasted from the middle of October till
near December, with scarcely a break. There were
six weeks of Indian summer, all gold by day, and,
when the moon came, all silver by night. The river
was so smooth at times as to be almost invisible, and
in its place was the indefinite continuation of the
opposite shore down toward the nether world. One
seemed to be in an enchanted land, and to breathe
all day the atmosphere of fable and romance. Not
a smoke, but a kind of shining nimbus filled all
the spaces. The vessels would drift by as if in
mid-air with all their sails set. The gypsy blood in
one, as Lowell calls it, could hardly stay between
four walls and see such days go by. Living in tents,
in groves and on the hills, seemed the only natural
life.

Late in December we had glimpses of the same
weather, — the earth had not yet passed all the
golden isles. On the 27th of that month, I find I
made this entry in my note-book: "A soft, hazy

day, the year asleep and dreaming of the Indian summer again. Not a breath of air and not a ripple on the river. The sunshine is hot as it falls across my table."

But what a terrible winter followed! what a savage chief the fair Indian maiden gave birth to!

This halcyon period of our autumn will always in some way be associated with the Indian. It is red and yellow and dusky like him. The smoke of his camp-fire seems again in the air. The memory of him pervades the woods. His plumes and moccasins and blanket of skins form just the costume the season demands. It was doubtless his chosen period. The gods smiled upon him then if ever. The time of the chase, the season of the buck and the doe, and of the ripening of all forest fruits; the time when all men are incipient hunters, when the first frosts have given pungency to the air, when to be abroad on the hills or in the woods is a delight that both old and young feel, — if the red aborigine ever had his summer of fullness and contentment, it must have been at this season, and it fitly bears his name.

In how many respects fall imitates or parodies the spring! It is indeed, in some of its features, a sort of second youth of the year. Things emerge and become conspicuous again. The trees attract all eyes as in May. The birds come forth from their summer privacy and parody their spring reunions and rivalries; some of them sing a little after

a silence of months. The robins, bluebirds, meadow-
larks, sparrows, crows, all sport, and call, and be-
have in a manner suggestive of spring. The cock
grouse drums in the woods as he did in April and
May. The pigeons reappear, and the wild geese
and ducks. The witch-hazel blooms. The trout
spawns. The streams are again full. The air is
humid, and the moisture rises in the ground. Nature is breaking camp, as in spring she was going
into camp. The spring yearning and restlessness
is represented in one by the increased desire to
travel.

Spring is the inspiration, fall the expiration.
Both seasons have their equinoxes, both their filmy,
hazy air, their ruddy forest tints, their cold rains,
their drenching fogs, their mystic moons; both have
the same solar light and warmth, the same rays of
the sun; yet, after all, how different the feelings
which they inspire! One is the morning, the other
the evening; one is youth, the other is age.

The difference is not merely in us; there is a
subtle difference in the air, and in the influences
that emanate upon us from the dumb forms of
nature. All the senses report a difference. The
sun seems to have burned out. One recalls the
notion of Herodotus that he is grown feeble, and
retreats to the south because he can no longer face
the cold and the storms from the north. There is a
growing potency about his beams in spring, a wan-

ing splendor about them in fall. One is the kindling fire, the other the subsiding flame.

It is rarely that an artist succeeds in painting unmistakably the difference between sunrise and sunset; and it is equally a trial of his skill to put upon canvas the difference between early spring and late fall, say between April and November. It was long ago observed that the shadows are more opaque in the morning than in the evening ; the struggle between the light and the darkness more marked, the gloom more solid, the contrasts more sharp. The rays of the morning sun chisel out and cut down the shadows in a way those of the setting sun do not. Then the sunlight is whiter and newer in the morning, — not so yellow and diffused. A difference akin to this is true of the two seasons I am speaking of. The spring is the morning sunlight, clear and determined ; the autumn, the afternoon rays, pensive, lessening, golden.

Does not the human frame yield to and sympathize with the seasons ? Are there not more births in the spring and more deaths in the fall ? In the spring one vegetates; his thoughts turn to sap; another kind of activity seizes him; he makes new wood which does not harden till past midsummer. For my part, I find all literary work irksome from April to August; my sympathies run in other channels ; the grass grows where meditation walked. As fall approaches, the currents mount to the head again. But my thoughts do not ripen well till after there has been a frost. The burrs will not open much before that. A man's thinking, I take it, is a kind of combustion, as is the ripening of fruits and leaves, and he wants plenty of oxygen in the air.

Then the earth seems to have become a positive magnet in the fall; the forge and anvil of the sun have had their effect. In the spring it is negative to all intellectual conditions, and drains one of his lightning.

To-day, October 21, I found the air in the bushy fields and lanes under the woods loaded with the perfume of the witch-hazel, — a sweetish, sickening odor. With the blooming of this bush, Nature says, "Positively the last." It is a kind of birth in death, of spring in fall, that impresses one as a little uncanny. All trees and shrubs form their flower-buds in the fall, and keep the secret till spring. How comes the witch-hazel to be the one exception, and to celebrate its floral nuptials on the funeral day of its foliage? No doubt it will be found that the spirit of some lovelorn squaw has passed into this bush, and that this is why it blooms in the Indian summer rather than in the white man's spring.

But it makes the floral series of the woods complete. Between it and the shad-blow of earliest spring lies the mountain of bloom; the latter at the

base on one side, this at the base on the other, with
the chestnut blossoms at the top in midsummer.

A peculiar feature of our fall may sometimes be
seen of a clear afternoon late in the season. Looking athwart the fields under the sinking sun, the
ground appears covered with a shining veil of gossamer. A fairy net, invisible at midday and which
the position of the sun now reveals, rests upon the
stubble and upon the spears of grass, covering acres
in extent, — the work of innumerable little spiders. The cattle walk through it, but do not seem to
break it. Perhaps a fly would make his mark upon
it. At the same time, stretching from the tops of
the trees, or from the top of a stake in the fence,
and leading off toward the sky, may be seen the
cables of the flying spider, — a fairy bridge from the
visible to the invisible. Occasionally seen against
a deep mass of shadow, and perhaps enlarged by
clinging particles of dust, they show quite plainly
and sag down like a stretched rope, or sway and
undulate like a hawser in the tide.

They recall a verse of our rugged poet, Walt
Whitman: —

" A noiseless patient spider,
I mark'd where, in a little promontory, it stood isolated:
Mark'd how, to explore the vacant, vast surrounding,
It launch'd forth filament, filament, filament out of it-
        self;
Ever unreeling them — ever tireless spreading them.

" And you, O my soul, where you stand,
Surrounded, surrounded, in measureless oceans of
    space,
Ceaselessly musing, venturing, throwing, —
Seeking the spheres to connect them;
Till the bridge you will need be formed — till the ductile
    anchor hold;
Till the gossamer thread you fling, catch somewhere, O
    my soul."

To return a little, September may be described
as the month of tall weeds. Where they have been
suffered to stand, along fences, by roadsides, and
in forgotten corners, — redroot, pigweed, ragweed,
vervain, goldenrod, burdock, elecampane, thistles,
teasels, nettles, asters, etc., — how they lift themselves up as if not afraid to be seen now! They are
all outlaws; every man's hand is against them; yet
how surely they hold their own! They love the
roadside, because here they are comparatively safe;
and ragged and dusty, like the common tramps
that they are, they form one of the characteristic
features of early fall.

I have often noticed in what haste certain weeds
are at times to produce their seeds. Redroot will
grow three or four feet high when it has the whole
season before it; but let it get a late start, let it
come up in August, and it scarcely gets above the
ground before it heads out, and apparently goes to
work with all its might and main to mature its

seed. In the growth of most plants or weeds, April
and May represent their root, June and July their
stalk, and August and September their flower
and seed. Hence, when the stalk months are stricken
out, as in the present case, there is only time for a
shallow root and a foreshortened head. I think
most weeds that get a late start show this curtail-
ment of stalk, and this solicitude to reproduce themselves. But I have not observed that any of the
cereals are so worldly wise. They have not had to
think and to shift for themselves as the weeds have.
It does indeed look like a kind of forethought in the
redroot. It is killed by the first frost, and hence
knows the danger of delay.

How rich in color, before the big show of the
tree foliage has commenced, our roadsides are in
places in early autumn, — rich to the eye that goes
hurriedly by and does not look too closely, — with
the profusion of goldenrod and blue and purple
asters dashed in upon here and there with the crimson leaves of the dwarf sumac ; and at intervals,
rising out of the fence corner or crowning a ledge
of rocks, the dark green of the cedar with the still
fire of the woodbine at its heart. I wonder if the
waysides of other lands present any analogous spec-
tacles at this season.

Then, when the maples have burst out into color,
showing like great bonfires along the hills, there is
indeed a feast for the eye. A maple before your

windows in October, when the sun shines upon it,
will make up for a good deal of the light it has
excluded; it fills the room with a soft golden glow.

Thoreau, I believe, was the first to remark upon
the individuality of trees of the same species with
respect to their foliage, — some maples ripening
their leaves early and some late, and some being of
one tint and some of another; and, moreover, that
each tree held to the same characteristics, year after
year. There is, indeed, as great a variety among the
maples as among the trees of an apple orchard;
some are harvest apples, some are fall apples, and
some are winter apples, each with a tint of its own.
Those late ripeners are the winter varieties, — the
Rhode Island greenings or swaars of their kind.
The red maple is the early astrachan. Then come
the red-streak, the yellow-sweet, and others. There
are windfalls among them, too, as among the apples,
and one side or hemisphere of the leaf is usually
brighter than the other.

The ash has been less noticed for its autumnal
foliage than it deserves. The richest shades of
plum-color to be seen — becoming by and by, or in
certain lights, a deep maroon — are afforded by this
tree. Then at a distance there seems to be a sort
of bloom on it, as upon the grape or plum. Amid
a grove of yellow maple, it makes a most pleasing
contrast.

By mid-October, most of the Rip Van Winkles

among our brute creatures have lain down for their winter nap. The toads and turtles have buried themselves in the earth. The woodchuck is in his hibernaculum, the skunk in his, the mole in his; and the black bear has his selected, and will go in when the snow comes. He does not like the looks of his big tracks in the snow. They publish his goings and comings too plainly. The coon retires about the same time. The provident wood-mice and the chipmunk are laying by a winter supply of nuts or grain, the former usually in decayed trees, the latter in the ground. I have observed that any unusual disturbance in the woods, near where the chipmunk has his den, will cause him to shift his quarters. One October, for many successive days, I saw one carrying into his hole buckwheat which he had stolen from a near field. The hole was only a few rods from where we were getting out stone, and as our work progressed, and the racket and uproar increased, the chipmunk became alarmed. He ceased carrying in, and after much hesitating and darting about, and some prolonged absences, he began to carry out; he had determined to move; if the mountain fell, he, at least, would be away in time. So, by mouthfuls or cheekfuls, the grain was transferred to a new place. He did not make a "bee" to get it done, but carried it all himself, occupying several days, and making a trip about every ten minutes.

The red and gray squirrels do not lay by winter
stores ; their cheeks are made without pockets, and
whatever they transport is carried in the teeth.
They are more or less active all winter, but October
and November are their festal months.   Invade
some butternut or hickory-nut grove on a frosty
October morning, and hear the red squirrel beat the
"juba" on a horizontal branch.   It is a most lively
jig, what the boys call a "regular break-down,"
interspersed with squeals and snickers and derisive
laughter. The most noticeable peculiarity about the
vocal part of it is the fact that it is a kind of duet.
In other words, by some ventriloquial tricks, he
appears to accompany himself, as if his voice split
up, a part forming a low guttural sound, and a part
a shrill nasal sound.

The distant bark of the more wary gray squirrel
may be heard about the same time.   There is a
teasing and ironical tone in it also, but the gray
squirrel is not the Puck the red is.

Insects also go into winter-quarters by or before
this time ; the bumble-bee, hornet, and wasp. But
here only royalty escapes; the queen-mother alone
foresees the night of winter coming and the morning
of spring beyond. The rest of the tribe try gypsy-
ing for a while, but perish in the first frosts. The
present October I surprised the queen of the yellow-
jackets in the woods looking out a suitable retreat.
The royal dame was house-hunting, and, on being

disturbed by my inquisitive poking among the leaves, she got up and flew away with a slow, deep hum. Her body was unusually distended, whether with fat or eggs I am unable to say. In September I took down the nest of the black hornet and found several large queens in it, but the workers had all gone. The queens were evidently weathering the first frosts and storms here, and waiting for the Indian summer to go forth and seek a permanent winter abode. If the covers could be taken off the fields and woods at this season, how many interesting facts of natural history would be revealed! — the crickets, ants, bees, reptiles, animals, and, for aught I know, the spiders and flies asleep or getting ready to sleep in their winter dormitories; the fires of life banked up, and burning just enough to keep the spark over till spring.

The fish all run down the stream in the fall except the trout; it runs up or stays up and spawns in November, the male becoming as brilliantly tinted as the deepest-dyed maple leaf. I have often wondered why the trout spawns in the fall, instead of in the spring like other fish. Is it not because a full supply of clear spring water can be counted on at that season more than at any other? The brooks are not so liable to be suddenly muddied by heavy showers, and defiled with the washings of the roads and fields, as they are in spring and summer. The artificial breeder finds that absolute purity of water

is necessary to hatch the spawn ; also that shade
and a low temperature are indispensable.

Our northern November day itself is like spring
water. It is melted frost, dissolved snow. There
is a chill in it and an exhilaration also. The forenoon is all morning and the afternoon all evening.
The shadows seem to come forth and to revenge
themselves upon the day. The sunlight is diluted
with darkness. The colors fade from the landscape,
and only the sheen of the river lights up the gray
and brown distance.

A BED OF BOUGHS

WHEN Aaron came again to camp and tramp with me, or, as he wrote, "to eat locusts and wild honey with me in the wilderness," it was past the middle of August, and the festival of the season neared its close. We were belated guests, but perhaps all the more eager on that account, especially as the country was suffering from a terrible drought, and the only promise of anything fresh or tonic or cool was in primitive woods and mountain passes.

"Now, my friend," said I, "we can go to Canada, or to the Maine woods, or to the Adirondacks, and thus have a whole loaf and a big loaf of this bread which you know as well as I will have heavy streaks in it, and will not be uniformly sweet; or we can seek nearer woods, and content ourselves with one week instead of four, with the prospect of a keen relish to the last. Four sylvan weeks sound well, but the poetry is mainly confined to the first one. We can take another slice or two of the Catskills, can we not, without being sated with kills and dividing ridges?"

"Anywhere," replied Aaron, "so that we have a good tramp and plenty of primitive woods. No doubt we should find good browsing on Peakamoose, and trout enough in the streams at its base."

So without further ado we made ready, and in due time found ourselves, with our packs on our backs, entering upon a pass in the mountains that led to the valley of the Rondout.

The scenery was wild and desolate in the extreme, the mountains on either hand looking as if they had been swept by a tornado of stone. Stone avalanches hung suspended on their sides, or had shot down into the chasm below. It was a kind of Alpine scenery, where crushed and broken boulders covered the earth instead of snow.

In the depressions in the mountains the rocky fragments seemed to have accumulated, and to have formed what might be called stone glaciers that were creeping slowly down.

Two hours' march brought us into heavy timber where the stone cataclysm had not reached, and before long the soft voice of the Rondout was heard in the gulf below us. We paused at a spring run, and I followed it a few yards down its mountain stairway, carpeted with black moss, and had my first glimpse of the unknown stream. I stood upon rocks and looked many feet down into a still, sunlit pool and saw the trout disporting themselves in the transparent water, and I was ready to encamp at once; but my companion, who had not been tempted by the view, insisted upon holding to our original purpose, which was to go farther up the stream. We passed a clearing with three or four houses and a saw-mill. The dam of the latter was filled with such clear water that it seemed very shallow, and not ten or twelve feet deep, as it really was. The fish were as conspicuous as if they had been in a pail.

Two miles farther up we suited ourselves and went into camp.

If there ever was a stream cradled in the rocks, detained lovingly by them, held and fondled in a rocky lap or tossed in rocky arms, that stream is the Rondout. Its course for several miles from its head is over the stratified rock, and into this it has worn a channel that presents most striking and peculiar features. Now it comes silently along on the top of the rock, spread out and flowing over that thick, dark green moss that is found only in the coldest streams; then drawn into a narrow canal only four or five feet wide, through which it shoots, black and rigid, to be presently caught in a deep basin with shelving, overhanging rocks, beneath which the phœbe-bird builds in security, and upon which the fisherman stands and casts his twenty or thirty feet of line without fear of being thwarted by the brush; then into a black, well-like pool, ten or fifteen feet deep, with a smooth, circular wall of rock on one side worn by the water through long ages; or else into a deep, oblong pocket, into which and out of which the water glides without a ripple.

The surface rock is a coarse sandstone superincumbent upon a lighter-colored conglomerate that looks like Shawangunk grits, and when this latter is reached by the water it seems to be rapidly disintegrated by it, thus forming the deep excavations alluded to.

My eyes had never before beheld such beauty in a mountain stream. The water was almost as transparent as the air, — was, indeed, like liquid air; and as it lay in these wells and pits enveloped in shadow, or lit up by a chance ray of the vertical sun, it was a perpetual feast to the eye, — so cool, so deep, so pure; every reach and pool like a vast spring. You lay down and drank or dipped the water up in your cup, and found it just the right degree of refreshing coldness. One is never prepared for the clearness of the water in these streams. It is always a surprise. See them every year for a dozen years, and yet, when you first come upon one, you will utter an exclamation. I saw nothing like it in the Adirondacks, nor in Canada. Absolutely without stain or hint of impurity, it seems to magnify like a lens, so that the bed of the stream and the fish in it appear deceptively near. It is rare to find even a trout stream that is not a little " off color," as they say of diamonds, but the waters in the section of which I am writing have the genuine ray; it is the undimmed and untarnished diamond.

If I were a trout, I should ascend every stream

till I found the Rondout. It is the ideal brook.
What homes these fish have, what retreats under
the rocks, what paved or flagged courts and areas,
what crystal depths where no net or snare can reach
them! — no mud, no sediment, but here and there
in the clefts and seams of the rock patches of white
gravel, — spawning-beds ready-made.

The finishing touch is given by the moss with
which the rock is everywhere carpeted. Even in
the narrow grooves or channels where the water runs
the swiftest, the green lining is unbroken. It sweeps
down under the stream and up again on the other
side, like some firmly woven texture. It softens
every outline and cushions every stone. At a certain depth in the great basins and wells it of course
ceases, and only the smooth-swept flagging of the
place-rock is visible.

The trees are kept well back from the margin of
the stream by the want of soil, and the large ones
unite their branches far above it, thus forming a
high winding gallery, along which the fisherman
passes and makes his long casts with scarcely an
interruption from branch or twig. In a few places
he makes no cast, but sees from his rocky perch the
water twenty feet below him, and drops his hook
into it as into a well.

We made camp at a bend in the creek where
there was a large surface of mossy rock uncovered
by the shrunken stream, — a clean, free space left

for us in the wilderness that was faultless as a kitchen
and dining-room, and a marvel of beauty as a loun-
ging-room, or an open court, or what you will. An
obsolete wood or bark road conducted us to it,
and disappeared up the hill in the woods beyond.
A loose boulder lay in the middle, and on the
edge next the stream were three or four large natural wash-basins scooped out of the rock, and ever
filled ready for use. Our lair we carved out of the
thick brush under a large birch on the bank. Here
we planted our flag of smoke and feathered our
nest with balsam and hemlock boughs and ferns,
and laughed at your four walls and pillows of
down.

Wherever one encamps in the woods, there is
home, and every object and feature about the place
take on a new interest and assume a near and
friendly relation to one.

We were at the head of the best fishing. There
was an old bark-clearing not far off which afforded
us a daily dessert of most delicious blackberries, —
an important item in the woods, — and then all the
features of the place — a sort of cave above ground
— were of the right kind.

There was not a mosquito, or gnat, or other pest
in the woods, the cool nights having already cut
them off. The trout were sufficiently abundant, and
afforded us a few hours' sport daily to supply our
wants. The only drawback was, that they were out

of season, and only palatable to a woodman's keen appetite. What is this about trout spawning in October and November, and in some cases not till March? These trout had all spawned in August, every one of them. The coldness and purity of the water evidently made them that much earlier. The game laws of the State protect the fish after September 1, proceeding upon the theory that its spawning season is later than that, — as it is in many cases, but not in all, as we found out.

The fish are small in these streams, seldom weighing over a few ounces. Occasionally a large one is seen of a pound or pound and a half weight. I remember one such, as black as night, that ran under a black rock. But I remember much more distinctly a still larger one that I caught and lost one eventful day.

I had him on my hook ten minutes, and actually got my thumb in his mouth, and yet he escaped.

It was only the over-eagerness of the sportsman. I imagined I could hold him by the teeth.

The place where I struck him was a deep well-hole, and I was perched upon a log that spanned it ten or twelve feet above the water. The situation was all the more interesting because I saw no possible way to land my fish. I could not lead him ashore, and my frail tackle could not be trusted to lift him sheer from that pit to my precarious perch. What should I do? call for help? but no help was near.

I had a revolver in my pocket and might have shot him through and through, but that novel proceeding did not occur to me until it was too late. I would have taken a Sam Patch leap into the water, and have wrestled with my antagonist in his own element, but I knew the slack, thus sure to occur, would probably free him; so I peered down upon the beautiful creature and enjoyed my triumph as far as it went. He was caught very lightly through his upper jaw, and I expected every struggle and somersault would break the hold. Presently I saw a place in the rocks where I thought it possible, with such an incentive, to get down within reach of the water: by careful manœuvring I slipped my pole behind me and got hold of the line, which I cut and wound around my finger; then I made my way toward the end of the log and the place in the rocks, leading my fish along much exhausted on the top of the water. By an effort worthy the occasion I got down within reach of the fish, and, as I have already confessed, thrust my thumb into his mouth and pinched his cheek; he made a spring and was free from my hand and the hook at the same time; for a moment he lay panting on the top of the water, then, recovering himself slowly, made his way down through the clear, cruel element beyond all hope of recapture. My blind impulse to follow and try to seize him was very strong, but I kept my hold and peered and peered long after the fish was lost to

view, then looked my mortification in the face and
laughed a bitter laugh.

" But, hang it! I had all the fun of catching the
fish, and only miss the pleasure of eating him, which
at this time would not be great."

" The fun, I take it," said my soldier, " is in tri-
umphing, and not in being beaten at the last."

" Well, have it so; but I would not exchange
those ten or fifteen minutes with that trout for the
tame two hours you have spent in catching that
string of thirty. To *see* a big fish after days of
small fry is an event; to have a jump from one is a
glimpse of the sportsman's paradise ; and to hook
one, and actually have him under your control for
ten minutes, — why, that is paradise itself as long
as it lasts."

One day I went down to the house of a settler
a mile below, and engaged the good dame to make
us a couple of loaves of bread, and in the evening
we went down after them. How elastic and exhila-
rating the walk was through the cool, transparent
shadows! The sun was gilding the mountains, and
its yellow light seemed to be reflected through all
the woods. At one point we looked through and
along a valley of deep shadow upon a broad sweep
of mountain quite near and densely clothed with
woods, flooded from base to summit by the setting
sun. It was a wild, memorable scene. What power
and effectiveness in Nature, I thought, and how

rarely an artist catches her touch! Looking down upon or squarely into a mountain covered with a heavy growth of birch and maple, and shone upon by the sun, is a sight peculiarly agreeable to me. How closely the swelling umbrageous heads of the trees fit together, and how the eye revels in the flowing and easy uniformity, while the mind feels the ruggedness and terrible power beneath!

As we came back, the light yet lingered on the top of Slide Mountain.

" ' The last that parleys with the setting sun,' "

said I, quoting Wordsworth.

" That line is almost Shakespearean," said my companion. " It suggests that great hand at least, though it has not the grit and virility of the more primitive bard. What triumph and fresh morning power in Shakespeare's lines that will occur to us at sunrise to-morrow! —

" 'And jocund day
Stands tiptoe on the misty mountain tops.'

Or in this : —

" ' Full many a glorious morning have I seen
Flatter the mountain tops with sovran eye.'

There is savage, perennial beauty there, the quality that Wordsworth and nearly all the modern poets lack."

" But Wordsworth is the poet of the mountains," said I, " and of lonely peaks. True, he does not express the power and aboriginal grace there is in them, nor toy with them and pluck them up by the hair of their heads, as Shakespeare does. There is something in Peakamoose yonder, as we see it from this point, cutting the blue vault with its dark, serrated edge, not in the bard of Grasmere; but he expresses the feeling of loneliness and insignificance that the cultivated man has in the presence of mountains, and the burden of solemn emotion they give rise to. Then there is something much more wild and merciless, much more remote from human interests and ends, in our long, high, wooded ranges than is expressed by the peaks and scarred groups of the lake country of Britain. These mountains we behold and cross are not picturesque, — they are wild and inhuman as the sea. In them you are in a maze, in a weltering world of woods; you can see neither the earth nor the sky, but a confusion of the growth and decay of centuries, and must traverse them by your compass or your science of woodcraft, — a rift through the trees giving one a glimpse of the opposite range or of the valley beneath, and he is more at sea than ever; one does not know his own farm or settlement when framed in these mountain treetops; all look alike unfamiliar."

Not the least of the charm of camping out is your camp-fire at night. What an artist! What pictures are boldly thrown or faintly outlined upon the canvas of the night! Every object, every attitude of

your companion is striking and memorable. You
see effects and groups every moment that you would
give money to be able to carry away with you in
enduring form. How the shadows leap, and skulk,
and hover about! Light and darkness are in perpetual tilt and warfare, with first the one unhorsed,
then the other. The friendly and cheering fire,
what acquaintance we make with it! We had almost forgotten there was such an element, we had so
long known only its dark offspring, heat. Now we
see the wild beauty uncaged and note its manner
and temper. How surely it creates its own draught
and sets the currents going, as force and enthusiasm always will! It carves itself a chimney out of
the fluid and houseless air. A friend, a minister-
ing angel, in subjection; a fiend, a fury, a monster,
ready to devour the world, if ungoverned. By day
it burrows in the ashes and sleeps; at night it comes
forth and sits upon its throne of rude logs, and rules
the camp, a sovereign queen.

Near camp stood a tall, ragged yellow birch, its
partially cast-off bark hanging in crisp sheets or
dense rolls.

" That tree needs the barber," we said, " and
shall have a call from him to-night."

So after dark I touched a match into it, and we
saw the flames creep up and wax in fury until the
whole tree and its main branches stood wrapped in
a sheet of roaring flame. It was a wild and strik-

ing spectacle, and must have advertised our camp to every nocturnal creature in the forest.

What does the camper think about when lounging around the fire at night? Not much, — of the sport of the day, of the big fish he lost and might have saved, of the distant settlement, of to-morrow's plans. An owl hoots off in the mountain and he thinks of him; if a wolf were to howl or a panther to scream, he would think of him the rest of the night. As it is, things flicker and hover through his mind, and he hardly knows whether it is the past or the present that possesses him. Certain it is, he feels the hush and solitude of the great forest, and, whether he will or not, all his musings are in some way cast upon that huge background of the night. Unless he is an old camper-out, there will be an undercurrent of dread or half fear. My companion said he could not help but feel all the time that there ought to be a sentinel out there pacing up and down. One seems to require less sleep in the woods, as if the ground and the untempered air rested and refreshed him sooner. The balsam and the hemlock heal his aches very quickly. If one is awakened often during the night, as he invariably is, he does not feel that sediment of sleep in his mind next day that he does when the same interruption occurs at home; the boughs have drawn it all out of him.

And it is wonderful how rarely any of the housed and tender white man's colds or influenzas come through these open doors and windows of the woods. It is our partial isolation from Nature that is dangerous; throw yourself unreservedly upon her and she rarely betrays you.

If one takes anything to the woods to read, he seldom reads it; it does not taste good with such primitive air.

There are very few camp poems that I know of, poems that would be at home with one on such an expedition; there is plenty that is weird and spectral, as in Poe, but little that is woody and wild as this scene is. I recall a Canadian poem by the late C. D. Shanly — the only one, I believe, the author ever wrote — that fits well the distended pupil of the mind's eye about the camp-fire at night. It was printed many years ago in the " Atlantic Monthly," and is called " The Walker of the Snow;" it begins thus: —

> " ' Speed on, speed on, good master;
>   The camp lies far away;
>   We must cross the haunted valley
>   Before the close of day.' ''

" That has a Canadian sound," said Aaron; " give us more of it."

> " ' How the snow-blight came upon me
>   I will tell you as we go, —
>   The blight of the shadow hunter
>   Who walks the midnight snow.'

And so on. The intent seems to be to personify
the fearful cold that overtakes and benumbs the
traveler in the great Canadian forests in winter.
This stanza brings out the silence or desolation of
the scene very effectively, — a scene without sound
or motion: —

> " ' Save the wailing of the moose-bird
>   With a plaintive note and low;
>   And the skating of the red leaf
>   Upon the frozen snow.'

" The rest of the poem runs thus: —

> " ' And said I, Though dark is falling,
>   And far the camp must be,
>   Yet my heart it would be lightsome
>   If I had but company.

> " ' And then I sang and shouted,
>   Keeping measure as I sped,
>   To the harp-twang of the snow-shoe
>   As it sprang beneath my tread.

> " ' Nor far into the valley
>   Had I dipped upon my way,
>   When a dusky figure joined me
>   In a capuchin of gray,

> " ' Bending upon the snow-shoes
>   With a long and limber stride ;
>   And I hailed the dusky stranger,
>   As we traveled side by side.

" ' But no token of communion
    Gave he by word or look,
And the fear-chill fell upon me
    At the crossing of the brook.

" ' For I saw by the sickly moonlight,
    As I followed, bending low,
That the walking of the stranger
    Left no foot-marks on the snow.

" ' Then the fear-chill gathered o'er me,
    Like a shroud around me cast,
As I sank upon the snow-drift
    Where the shadow hunter passed.

" ' And the otter-trappers found me,
    Before the break of day,
With my dark hair blanched and whitened
    As the snow in which I lay.

" ' But they spoke not as they raised me ;
    For they knew that in the night
I had seen the shadow hunter
    And had withered in his sight.

" ' Sancta Maria speed us!
    The sun is fallen low:
Before us lies the valley
    Of the Walker of the Snow!' "

" Ah!" exclaimed my companion. " Let us pile
on more of those dry birch-logs; I feel both the

'fear-chill' and the 'cold-chill' creeping over me.
How far is it to the valley of the Neversink?"

"About three or four hours' march, the man
said."

"I hope we have no haunted valleys to cross?"

"None," said I, "but we pass an old log cabin
about which there hangs a ghostly superstition. At
a certain hour in the night, during the time the bark
is loose on the hemlock, a female form is said to
steal from it and grope its way into the wilderness.
The tradition runs that her lover, who was a bark-
peeler and wielded the spud, was killed by his rival,
who felled a tree upon him while they were at
work. The girl, who helped her mother cook for the
'hands,' was crazed by the shock, and that night stole
forth into the woods and was never seen or heard
of more. There are old hunters who aver that her
cry may still be heard at night at the head of the
valley whenever a tree falls in the stillness of the
forest."

"Well, I heard a tree fall not ten minutes ago,"
said Aaron; "a distant, rushing sound with a subdued crash at the end of it, and the only answering
cry I heard was the shrill voice of the screech owl
off yonder against the mountain. But maybe it
was not an owl," said he after a moment; "let us
help the legend along by believing it was the voice
of the lost maiden."

"By the way," continued he, "do you remember

the pretty creature we saw seven years ago in the
shanty on the West Branch, who was really helping
her mother cook for the hands, a slip of a girl twelve
or thirteen years old, with eyes as beautiful and
bewitching as the waters that flowed by her cabin?
I was wrapped in admiration till she spoke; then
how the spell was broken! Such a voice! It was
like the sound of pots and pans when you expected
to hear a lute."

The next day we bade farewell to the Rondout,
and set out to cross the mountain to the east branch
of the Neversink.

"We shall find tame waters compared with these,
I fear, — a shriveled stream brawling along over
loose stones, with few pools or deep places."

Our course was along the trail of the bark-men
who had pursued the doomed hemlock to the last
tree at the head of the valley. As we passed along,
a red steer stepped out of the bushes into the road
ahead of us, where the sunshine fell full upon him,
and, with a half-scared, beautiful look, begged alms
of salt. We passed the Haunted Shanty; but both
it and the legend about it looked very tame at ten
o'clock in the morning. After the road had faded
out, we took to the bed of the stream to avoid the
gauntlet of the underbrush, skipping up the mountain from boulder to boulder. Up and up we went,
with frequent pauses and copious quaffing of the
cold water. My soldier declared a "haunted val-

ley" would be a godsend; anything but endless dragging of one's self up such an Alpine stairway. The winter wren, common all through the woods, peeped and scolded at us as we sat blowing near the summit, and the oven-bird, not quite sure as to what manner of creatures we were, hopped down a limb to within a few feet of us and had a good look, then darted off into the woods to tell the news. I also noted the Canada warbler, the chestnut-sided warbler, and the black-throated blue-back, — the latter most abundant of all. Up these mountain brooks, too, goes the belted kingfisher, swooping around through the woods when he spies the fisherman, then wheeling into the open space of the stream and literally making a "blue streak" down under the branches.

At last the stream which had been our guide was lost under the rocks, and before long the top was gained. These mountains are horse-shaped. There is always a broad, smooth back, more or less depressed, which the hunter aims to bestride; rising rapidly from this is pretty sure to be a rough, curving ridge that carries the forest up to some highest peak. We were lucky in hitting the saddle, but we could see a little to the south the sharp, steep neck of the steed sweeping up toward the sky with an erect mane of balsam fir.

These mountains are steed-like in other respects: any timid and vacillating course with them is sure to get you into trouble. One must strike out boldly, and not be disturbed by the curveting and shying; the valley you want lies squarely behind them, but farther off than you think, and if you do not go for it resolutely, you will get bewildered and the mountain will play you a trick.

I may say that Aaron and I kept a tight rein and a good pace till we struck a water-course on the other side, and that we clattered down it with no want of decision till it emptied into a larger stream which we knew must be the East Branch. An abandoned fishpole lay on the stones, marking the farthest point reached by some fisherman. According to our reckoning, we were five or six miles above the settlement, with a good depth of primitive woods all about us.

We kept on down the stream, now and then pausing at a likely place to take some trout for dinner, and with an eye out for a good camping-ground. Many of the trout were full of ripe spawn, and a few had spawned, the season with them being a little later than on the stream we had left, perhaps because the water was less cold. Neither had the creek here any such eventful and startling career. It led, indeed, quite a humdrum sort of life under the roots and fallen treetops and among the loose stones. At rare intervals it beamed upon us from some still reach or dark cover, and won from us our best attention in return.

The day was quite spent before we had pitched our air-woven tent and prepared our dinner, and we gathered boughs for our bed in the gloaming. Breakfast had to be caught in the morning and was not served early, so that it was nine o'clock before we were in motion. A little bird, the red-eyed vireo, warbled most cheerily in the trees above our camp, and, as Aaron said, "gave us a good send-off." We kept down the stream, following the inevitable bark road.

My companion had refused to look at another "dividing ridge" that had neither path nor way, and henceforth I must keep to the open road or travel alone. Two hours' tramp brought us to an old clearing with some rude, tumble-down log buildings that many years before had been occupied by the bark and lumber men. The prospect for trout was so good in the stream hereabouts, and the scene so peaceful and inviting, shone upon by the dreamy August sun, that we concluded to tarry here until the next day. It was a page of pioneer history opened to quite unexpectedly. A dim footpath led us a few yards to a superb spring, in which a trout from the near creek had taken up his abode. We took possession of what had been a shingle-shop, attracted by its huge fireplace. We floored it with balsam boughs, hung its walls with our "traps," and sent the smoke curling again from its disused chimney.

The most musical and startling sound we heard in the woods greeted our ears that evening about sundown as we sat on a log in front of our quarters, — the sound of slow, measured pounding in the valley below us. We did not know how near we were to human habitations, and the report of the lumberman's mallet, like the hammering of a great woodpecker, was music to the ear and news to the mind. The air was still and dense, and the silence such as alone broods over these little openings in the primitive woods. My soldier started as if he had heard a signal-gun. The sound, coming so far through the forest, sweeping over those great wind-harps of trees, became wild and legendary, though probably made by a lumberman driving a wedge or working about his mill.

We expected a friendly visit from porcupines that night, as we saw where they had freshly gnawed all about us; hence, when a red squirrel came and looked in upon us very early in the morning and awoke us by his snickering and giggling, my comrade cried out, " There is your porcupig." How the frisking red rogue seemed to enjoy what he had found! He looked in at the door and snickered, then in at the window, then peeked down from between the rafters and cachinnated till his sides must have ached; then struck an attitude upon the chimney, and fairly squealed with mirth and ridicule. In fact, he grew so obstreperous, and so disturbed our repose, that we had to " shoo " him away with one of our boots. He declared most plainly that he had never before seen so preposterous a figure as we cut lying there in the corner of that old shanty.

The morning boded rain, the week to which we had limited ourselves drew near its close, and we concluded to finish our holiday worthily by a good square tramp to the railroad station, twenty-three miles distant, as it proved. Two miles brought us to stumpy fields, and to the house of the upper inhabitant. They told us there was a short cut across the mountain, but my soldier shook his head.

" Better twenty miles of Europe," said he, getting Tennyson a little mixed, " than one of Cathay, or Slide Mountain either."

Drops of the much-needed rain began to come down, and I hesitated in front of the woodshed.

" Sprinkling weather always comes to some bad end," said Aaron, with a reminiscence of an old couplet in his mind, and so it proved, for it did not get beyond a sprinkle, and the sun shone out before noon.

In the next woods I picked up from the middle of the road the tail and one hind leg of one of our native rats, the first I had ever seen except in a museum. An owl or fox had doubtless left it the night before. It was evident the fragments had once formed part of a very elegant and slender creature. The fur that remained (for it was not hair)

was tipped with red. My reader doubtless knows
that the common rat is an importation, and that
there is a native American rat, usually found much
farther south than the locality of which I am writing, that lives in the woods, — a sylvan rat, very
wild and nocturnal in his habits, and seldom seen
even by hunters or woodmen. Its eyes are large
and fine, and its form slender. It looks like only
a far-off undegenerate cousin of the filthy creature
that has come to us from the long-peopled Old
World. Some creature ran between my feet and
the fire toward morning, the last night we slept
in the woods, and I have little doubt it was one of
these wood-rats.

The people in these back settlements are almost
as shy and furtive as the animals. Even the men
look a little scared when you stop them by your
questions. The children dart behind their parents
when you look at them. As we sat on a bridge resting, — for our packs still weighed fifteen or twenty
pounds each, — two women passed us with pails on
their arms, going for blackberries. They filed by
with their eyes down like two abashed nuns.

In due time we found an old road, to which we
had been directed, that led over the mountain to
the West Branch. It was a hard pull, sweetened
by blackberries and a fine prospect. The snowbird
was common along the way, and a solitary wild
pigeon shot through the woods in front of us, recall-

ing the nests we had seen on the East Branch, — little scaffoldings of twigs scattered all through the trees.

It was nearly noon when we struck the West Branch, and the sun was scalding hot. We knew that two and three pound trout had been taken there, and yet we wet not a line in its waters. The scene was primitive, and carried one back to the days of his grandfather, stumpy fields, log fences, log houses and barns. A boy twelve or thirteen years old came out of a house ahead of us eating a piece of bread and butter. We soon overtook him and held converse with him. He knew the land well, and what there was in the woods and the waters. He had walked out to the railroad station, fourteen miles distant, to see the cars, and back the same day. I asked him about the flies and mosquitoes, etc. He said they were all gone except the "blunder-heads;" there were some of them left yet.

"What are blunder-heads?" I inquired, sniffing new game.

"The pesky little fly that gets into your eye when you are a-fishing."

Ah, yes! I knew him well. We had got acquainted some days before, and I thanked the boy for the name. It is an insect that hovers before your eye as you thread the streams, and you are forever vaguely brushing at it under the delusion that it is a little spider suspended from your hat-brim; and just as you want to see clearest, into your eye it goes, head and ears, and is caught between the lids. You miss your cast, but you catch a " blunder-head."

We paused under a bridge at the mouth of Biscuit Brook and ate our lunch, and I can recommend it to be as good a wayside inn as the pedestrian need look for. Better bread and milk than we had there I never expect to find. The milk was indeed so good that Aaron went down to the little log house under the hill a mile farther on and asked for more; and being told they had no cow, he lingered five minutes on the doorstone with his sooty pail in his hand, putting idle questions about the way and distance to the mother while he refreshed himself with the sight of a well-dressed and comely-looking young girl, her daughter.

" I got no milk," said he, hurrying on after me, " but I got something better, only I cannot divide it."

" I know what it is," replied I; " I heard her voice."

" Yes, and it was a good one, too. The sweetest sound I ever heard," he went on, " was a girl's voice after I had been four years in the army, and, by Jove! if I did n't experience something of the same pleasure in hearing this young girl speak after a week in the woods. She had evidently been out in the world and was home on a visit. It was a different look she gave me from that of the natives. This is better than fishing for trout," said he. "You drop in at the next house."

But the next house looked too unpromising.

" There is no milk there," said I, " unless they keep a goat."

" But could we not," said my facetious companion, " go it on that?"

A couple of miles beyond I stopped at a house that enjoyed the distinction of being clapboarded, and had the good fortune to find both the milk and the young lady. A mother and her daughter were again the only occupants save a babe in the cradle, which the young woman quickly took occasion to disclaim.

" It has not opened its dear eyes before since its mother left. Come to aunty," and she put out her hands.

The daughter filled my pail and the mother replenished our stock of bread. They asked me to sit and cool myself, and seemed glad of a stranger to talk with. They had come from an adjoining county five years before, and had carved their little clearing out of the solid woods.

" The men folks," the mother said, " came on ahead and built the house right among the big trees," pointing to the stumps near the door.

One no sooner sets out with his pack upon his back to tramp through the land than all objects and persons by the way have a new and curious interest to him. The tone of his entire being is not a little elevated, and all his perceptions and susceptibilities quickened. I feel that some such statement is necessary to justify the interest that I felt in this backwoods maiden. A slightly pale face it was, strong and well arched, with a tender, wistful expression not easy to forget.

I had surely seen that face many times before in towns and cities, and in other lands, but I hardly expected to meet it here amid the stumps. What were the agencies that had given it its fine lines and its gracious intelligence amid these simple, primitive scenes? What did my heroine read, or think? or what were her unfulfilled destinies? She wore a sprig of prince's pine in her hair, which gave a touch peculiarly welcome.

" Pretty lonely," she said, in answer to my inquiry; " only an occasional fisherman in summer, and in winter — nobody at all."

And the little new schoolhouse in the woods farther on, with its half-dozen scholars and the girlish face of the teacher seen through the open door, — nothing less than the exhilaration of a journey on foot could have made it seem the interesting object it was. Two of the little girls had been to the spring after a pail of water, and came struggling out of the woods into the road with it as we passed. They set down their pail and regarded us with a half-curious, half-alarmed look.

" What is your teacher's name ? " asked one of us.

" Miss Lucinde Josephine ——— " began the red-haired one, then hesitated, bewildered, when the bright, dark-eyed one cut her short with " Miss Simms," and taking hold of the pail said, " Come on."

"Are there any scholars from above here ? " I inquired.

" Yes, Bobbie and Matie," and they hastened toward the door.

We once more stopped under a bridge for refreshments, and took our time, knowing the train would not go on without us. By four o'clock we were across the mountain, having passed from the watershed of the Delaware into that of the Hudson. The next eight miles we had a down grade but a rough road, and during the last half of it we had blisters on the bottoms of our feet. It is one of the rewards of the pedestrian that, however tired he may be, he is always more or less refreshed by his journey. His physical tenement has taken an airing. His respiration has been deepened, his circulation quickened. A good draught has carried off the fumes and the vapors. One's quality is intensified; the color strikes in. At noon that day I was much fatigued; at night I was leg-weary and footsore, but a fresh, hardy feeling had taken possession of me that lasted for weeks.

A TASTE OF MAINE BIRCH

THE traveler and camper-out in Maine, unless
he penetrates its more northern portions, has
less reason to remember it as a pine-tree State than
a birch-tree State. The white-pine forests have
melted away like snow in the spring and gone down-
stream, leaving only patches here and there in the
more remote and inaccessible parts. The portion of
the State I saw — the valley of the Kennebec and
the woods about Moxie Lake — had been shorn of
its pine timber more than forty years before, and
is now covered with a thick growth of spruce and
cedar and various deciduous trees. But the birch
abounds. Indeed, when the pine goes out the birch
comes in; the race of men succeeds the race of
giants. This tree has great stay-at-home virtues.
Let the sombre, aspiring, mysterious pine go; the
birch has humble, every-day uses. In Maine, the
paper or canoe birch is turned to more account than
any other tree. I read in Gibbon that the natives
of ancient Assyria used to celebrate in verse or
prose the three hundred and sixty uses to which
the various parts and products of the palm-tree were

applied. The Maine birch is turned to so many accounts that it may well be called the palm of this region. Uncle Nathan, our guide, said it was made especially for the camper-out ; yes, and for the woodman and frontiersman generally. It is a magazine, a furnishing store set up in the wilderness, whose goods are free to every comer. The whole equipment of the camp lies folded in it, and comes forth at the beck of the woodman's axe: tent, waterproof roof, boat, camp utensils, buckets, cups, plates, spoons, napkins, table-cloths, paper for letters or your journal, torches, candles, kindling-wood, and fuel. The canoe birch yields you its vestments with the utmost liberality. Ask for its coat, and it gives you its waistcoat also. Its bark seems wrapped about it layer upon layer, and comes off with great ease. We saw many rude structures and cabins shingled and sided with it, and haystacks capped with it. Near a maple-sugar camp there was a large pile of birch-bark sap-buckets, — each bucket made of a piece of bark about a yard square, folded up as the tinman folds up a sheet 'of tin to make a square vessel, the corners bent around against the sides and held by a wooden pin. When, one day, we were overtaken by a shower in traveling through the woods, our guide quickly stripped large sheets of the bark from a near tree, and we had each a perfect umbrella as by magic. When the rain was over, and we moved on, I wrapped mine about me like a large leather apron, and it shielded my clothes from the wet bushes. When we came to a spring, Uncle Nathan would have a birch-bark cup ready before any of us could get a tin one out of his knapsack, and I think water never tasted so sweet as from one of these bark cups. It is exactly the thing. It just fits the mouth, and it seems to give new virtues to the water. It makes me thirsty now when I think of it. In our camp at Moxie, we made a large birch-bark box to keep the butter in; and the butter in this box, covered with some leafy boughs, I think improved in flavor day by day. Maine butter needs something to mollify and sweeten it a little, and I think birch bark will do it. In camp Uncle Nathan often drank his tea and coffee from a bark cup; the china closet in the birch-tree was always handy, and our vulgar tinware was generally a good deal mixed, and the kitchen maid not at all particular about dish-washing. We all tried the oatmeal with the maple syrup in one of these dishes, and the stewed mountain cranberries, using a birch-bark spoon, and never found service better. Uncle Nathan declared he could boil potatoes in a bark kettle, and I did not doubt him. Instead of sending our soiled napkins and table-spreads to the wash, we rolled them up into candles and torches, and drew daily upon our stores in the forest for new ones.

But the great triumph of the birch is, of course,

the bark canoe. When Uncle Nathan took us out under his little woodshed, and showed us, or rather modestly permitted us to see, his nearly finished canoe, it was like a first glimpse of some new and unknown genius of the woods or streams. It sat there on the chips and shavings and fragments of bark like some shy, delicate creature just emerged from its hiding-place, or like some wild flower just opened. It was the first boat of the kind I had ever seen, and it filled my eye completely. What woodcraft it indicated, and what a wild, free life, sylvan life, it promised! It had such a fresh, ab-original look as I had never before seen in any kind of handiwork. Its clear, yellow-red color would have become the cheek of an Indian maiden. Then its supple curves and swells, its sinewy stays and thwarts, its bow-like contour, its tomahawk stem and stern rising quickly and sharply from its frame, were all vividly suggestive of the race from which it came. An old Indian had taught Uncle Nathan the art, and the soul of the ideal red man looked out of the boat before us. Uncle Nathan had spent two days ranging the mountains looking for a suit-able tree, and had worked nearly a week on the craft. It was twelve feet long, and would seat and carry five men nicely. Three trees contribute to the making of a canoe, beside the birch, namely, the white cedar for ribs and lining, the spruce for roots and fibres to sew its joints and bind its frame, and the pine for pitch or rosin to stop its seams and cracks. It is hand-made and home-made, or rather wood-made, in a sense that no other craft is, except a dugout, and it suggests a taste and a refinement that few products of civilization realize. The design of a savage, it yet looks like the thought of a poet, and its grace and fitness haunt the imagination. I suppose its production was the inevitable result of the Indian's wants and surroundings, but that does not detract from its beauty. It is, indeed, one of the fairest flowers the thorny plant of necessity ever bore. Our canoe, as I have intimated, was not yet finished when we first saw it, nor yet when we took it up, with its architect, upon our metaphorical backs and bore it to the woods. It lacked part of its cedar lining and the rosin upon its joints, and these were added after we reached our destination.

Though we were not indebted to the birch-tree for our guide, Uncle Nathan, as he was known in all that country, yet he matched well these woodsy products and conveniences. The birch-tree had given him a large part of his tuition, and, kneeling in his canoe and making it shoot noiselessly over the water with that subtle yet indescribably expressive and athletic play of the muscles of the back and shoulders, the boat and the man seemed born of the same spirit. He had been a hunter and trapper for over forty years ; he had grown gray in the woods, had ripened and matured there, and everything about him was as if the spirit of the woods had had the ordering of it ; his whole make-up was in a minor and subdued key, like the moss and the lichens, or like the protective coloring of the game, — everything but his quick sense and penetrative glance. He was as gentle and modest as a girl ; his sensibilities were like plants that grow in the shade. The woods and the solitudes had touched him with their own softening and refining influence ; had, indeed, shed upon his soil of life a rich, deep leaf mould that was delightful, and that nursed, half concealed, the tenderest and wildest growths. There was grit enough back of and beneath it all, but he presented none of the rough and repelling traits of character of the conventional backwoodsman. In the spring he was a driver of logs on the Kennebec, usually having charge of a large gang of men; in the winter he was a solitary trapper and hunter in the forests.

Our first glimpse of Maine waters was Pleasant Pond, which we found by following a white, rapid, musical stream from the Kennebec three miles back into the mountains. Maine waters are for the most part dark-complexioned, Indian-colored streams, but Pleasant Pond is a pale-face among them both in name and nature. It is the only strictly silver lake I ever saw. Its waters seem almost artificially white and brilliant, though of remarkable transpar-

ency. I think I detected minute shining motes held
in suspension in it. As for the trout, they are veritable bars of silver until you have cut their flesh, when
they are the reddest of gold. They have no crimson or other spots, and the straight lateral line is
but a faint pencil-mark. They appeared to be a
species of lake trout peculiar to these waters, uniformly from ten to twelve inches in length. And
these beautiful fish, at the time of our visit (last
of August) at least, were to be taken only in deep
water upon a hook baited with salt pork. And
then you needed a letter of introduction to them.
They were not to be tempted or cajoled by strangers. We did not succeed in raising a fish, although
instructed how it was to be done, until one of the
natives, a young and obliging farmer living hard
by, came and lent his countenance to the enterprise. I sat in one end of the boat and he in the
other, my pork was the same as his, and I manœu-
vred it as directed, and yet those fish knew his hook
from mine in sixty feet of water, and preferred it
four times in five. Evidently they did not bite because they were hungry, but solely for old acquaintance' sake.

Pleasant Pond is an irregular sheet of water, two
miles or more in its greatest diameter, with high
rugged mountains rising up from its western shore,
and low rolling hills sweeping back from its eastern
and northern, covered by a few sterile farms. I

was never tired, when the wind was still, of floating along its margin and gazing down into its marvelously translucent depths. The boulders and fragments of rocks were seen, at a depth of twenty-five or thirty feet, strewing its floor, and apparently as free from any covering of sediment as when they were dropped there by the old glaciers æons ago. Our camp was amid a dense grove of second growth of white pine on the eastern shore, where, for one, I found a most admirable cradle in a little depression outside of the tent, carpeted with pine needles, in which to pass the night. The camper-out is always in luck if he can find, sheltered by the trees, a soft hole in the ground, even if he has a stone for a pillow. The earth must open its arms a little for us even in life, if we are to sleep well upon its bosom. I have often heard my grandfather, who was a soldier of the Revolution, tell with great gusto how he once bivouacked in a little hollow made by the overturning of a tree, and slept so soundly that he did not wake up till his cradle was half full of water from a passing shower.

What bird or other creature might represent the divinity of Pleasant Pond I do not know, but its demon, as of most northern inland waters, is the loon; and a very good demon he is, too, suggesting something not so much malevolent as arch, sardonic, ubiquitous, circumventing, with just a tinge of something inhuman and uncanny. His fiery-red eyes gleaming forth from that jet-black head are full of meaning. Then his strange horse-laughter by day, and his weird, doleful cry at night, like that of a lost and wandering spirit, recall no other bird or beast. He suggests something almost supernatural in his alertness and amazing quickness, cheating the shot and the bullet of the sportsman out of their aim. I know of but one other bird so quick, and that is the hummingbird, which I never have been able to kill with a gun. The loon laughs the shotgun to scorn, and the obliging young farmer above referred to told me he had shot at them hundreds of times with his rifle, without effect, — they always dodged his bullet. We had in our party a breech-loading rifle, which weapon is perhaps an appreciable moment of time quicker than the ordinary muzzle-loader, and this the poor loon could not or did not dodge. He had not timed himself to that species of firearms, and when, with his fellow, he swam about within rifle range of our camp, letting off volleys of his wild, ironical *ha-ha*, he little suspected the dangerous gun that was matched against him. As the rifle cracked, both loons made the gesture of diving, but only one of them disappeared beneath the water; and when he came to the surface in a few moments, a hundred or more yards away, and saw his companion did not follow, but was floating on the water where he had last seen him, he took the alarm and sped away in the distance. The bird I had killed was a magnificent specimen, and I looked him over with great interest. His glossy checkered coat, his banded neck, his snow-white breast, his powerful lance-shaped beak, his red eyes, his black, thin, slender, marvelously delicate feet and legs, issuing from his muscular thighs, and looking as if they had never touched the ground, his strong wings well forward, while his legs were quite at the apex, and the neat, elegant model of the entire bird, speed and quickness and strength stamped upon every feature, — all delighted and lingered in the eye. The loon appears like anything but a silly bird, unless you see him in some collection, or in the shop of the taxidermist, where he usually looks very tame and goose-like. Nature never meant the loon to stand up, or to use his feet and legs for other purposes than swimming. Indeed, he cannot stand except upon his tail in a perpendicular attitude; but in the collections he is poised upon his feet like a barnyard fowl, all the wildness and grace and alertness gone out of him. My specimen sits upon a table as upon the surface of the water, his feet trailing behind him, his body low and trim, his head elevated and slightly turned as if in the act of bringing that fiery eye to bear upon you, and vigilance and power stamped upon every lineament.

The loon is to the fishes what the hawk is to the birds; he swoops down to unknown depths upon them, and not even the wary trout can elude him. Uncle Nathan said he had seen the loon disappear, and in a moment come up with a large trout, which he would cut in two with his strong beak and swallow piecemeal. Neither the loon nor the otter can bolt a fish under the water; he must come to the surface to dispose of it. (I once saw a man eat a cake under water in London.) Our guide told me he had seen the parent loon swimming with a single young one upon its back. When closely pressed, it dived, or "div," as he would have it, and left the young bird sitting upon the water. Then it too disappeared, and when the old one returned and called, it came out from the shore. On the wing overhead the loon looks not unlike a very large duck, but when it alights, it plows into the water like a bombshell. It probably cannot take flight from the land, as the one Gilbert White saw and describes in his letters was picked up in a field, unable to launch itself into the air.

From Pleasant Pond we went seven miles through the woods to Moxie Lake, following an overgrown lumberman's "tote" road, our canoe and supplies hauled on a sled by the young farmer with his three-year-old steers. I doubt if birch-bark ever made a rougher voyage than that. As I watched it above the bushes, the sled and the luggage being hidden, it appeared as if tossed in the wildest and most tempestuous sea. When the bushes closed above it, I felt as if it had gone down, or been broken into a hundred pieces. Billows of rocks and logs, and chasms of creeks and spring runs, kept it rearing and pitching in the most frightful manner. The steers went at a spanking pace; indeed, it was a regular bovine gale; but their driver clung to their side amid the brush and boulders with desperate tenacity, and seemed to manage them by signs and nudges, for he hardly uttered his orders aloud. But we got through without any serious mishap, passing Mosquito Creek and Mosquito Pond, and flanking Mosquito Mountain, but seeing no mosquitoes, and brought up at dusk at a lumberman's old hay-barn, standing in the midst of a lonely clearing on the shores of Moxie Lake.

Here we passed the night, and were lucky in having a good roof over our heads, for it rained heavily. After we were rolled in our blankets and variously disposed upon the haymow, Uncle Nathan lulled us to sleep by a long and characteristic yarn.

I had asked him, half jocosely, if he believed in "spooks;" but he took my question seriously, and without answering it directly, proceeded to tell us what he himself had known and witnessed. It was, by the way, extremely difficult either to surprise or to steal upon any of Uncle Nathan's private opinions and beliefs about matters and things. He was as shy of all debatable subjects as a fox is of a trap. He usually talked in a circle, just as he hunted moose and caribou, so as not to approach his point too rudely and suddenly. He would keep on the lee side of his interlocutor in spite of all one could do. He was thoroughly good and reliable, but the wild creatures of the woods, in pursuit of which he had spent so much of his life, had taught him a curious gentleness and indirection, and to keep himself in the background; he was careful that you should not scent his opinions upon any subject at all polemic, but he would tell you what he had seen and known. What he had seen and known about spooks was briefly this : In company with a neighbor he was passing the night with an old recluse who lived somewhere in these woods. Their host was an Englishman, who had the reputation of having murdered his wife some years before in another part of the country, and, deserted by his grown-up children, was eking out his days in poverty amid these solitudes. The three men were sleeping upon the floor, with Uncle Nathan next to a rude partition that divided the cabin into two rooms. At his head there was a door that opened into this other apartment. Late at night, Uncle Nathan said, he awoke and turned over, and his mind was occupied with various things, when he heard somebody behind the partition. He reached over and felt that both of his companions were in their places beside him, and he was somewhat surprised. The person, or whatever it was, in the other room moved about heavily, and pulled the table from its place beside the wall to the middle of the floor. "I was not dreaming," said Uncle Nathan; "I felt of my eyes twice to make sure, and they were wide open." Presently the door opened; he was sensible of the draught upon his head, and a woman's form stepped heavily past him; he felt the "swirl" of her skirts as she went by. Then there was a loud noise in the room, as if some one had fallen his whole length upon the floor. "It jarred the house," said he, "and woke everybody up. I asked old Mr. —— if he heard that noise. 'Yes,' said he, 'it was thunder.' But it was not thunder, I know that;" and then added, "I was no more afraid than I am this minute. I never was the least mite afraid in my life. And my eyes were wide open," he repeated; "I felt of them twice; but whether that was the speret of that man's murdered wife or not, I cannot tell. They said she was an uncommon heavy woman." Uncle Nathan was a man of unusually quick and acute senses, and he did not doubt their evidence on this occasion any more than he did when they prompted him to level his rifle at a bear or a moose.

Moxie Lake lies much lower than Pleasant Pond, and its waters compared with those of the latter are as copper compared with silver. It is very irregular in shape; now narrowing to the dimensions of a slow-moving grassy creek, then expand-

ing into a broad deep basin with rocky shores,
and commanding the noblest mountain scenery. It
is rarely that the pond-lily and the speckled trout
are found together, — the fish the soul of the purest
spring water, the flower the transfigured spirit of the
dark mud and slime of sluggish summer streams
and ponds ; yet in Moxie they were both found in
perfection. Our camp was amid the birches, poplars, and white cedars near the head of the lake,
where the best fishing at this season was to be
had. Moxie has a small oval head, rather shallow,
but bumpy with rocks ; a long, deep neck, full
of springs, where the trout lie ; and a very broad
chest, with two islands tufted with pine-trees for
breasts. We swam in the head, we fished in the
neck, or in a small section of it, a space about the
size of the Adam's apple, and we paddled across
and around the broad expanse below. Our birch-
bark was not finished and christened till we reached
Moxie. The cedar lining was completed at Pleasant Pond, where we had the use of a *bateau*, but
the rosin was not applied to the seams till we
reached this lake. When I knelt down in it for the
first time, and put its slender maple paddle into
the water, it sprang away with such quickness and
speed that it disturbed me in my seat. I had
spurred a more restive and spirited steed than I
was used to. In fact, I had never been in a craft
that sustained so close a relation to my will, and

was so responsive to my slightest wish. When I caught my first large trout from it, it sympathized a little too closely, and my enthusiasm started a leak, which, however, with a live coal and a piece of rosin, was quickly mended. You cannot perform much of a war-dance in a birch-bark canoe; better wait till you get on dry land. Yet as a boat it is not so shy and "ticklish" as I had imagined. One needs to be on the alert, as becomes a sportsman and an angler, and in his dealings with it must charge himself with three things, — precision, moderation, and circumspection.

Trout weighing four and five pounds have been taken at Moxie, but none of that size came to our hand. I realized the fondest hopes I had dared to indulge in when I hooked the first two-pounder of my life, and my extreme solicitude lest he get away I trust was pardonable. My friend, in relating the episode in camp, said I had implored him to row me down in the middle of the lake that I might have room to manœuvre my fish. But the slander has barely a grain of truth in it. The water near us showed several old stakes broken off just below the surface, and my fish was determined to wrap my leader about one of these stakes; it was only for the clear space a few yards farther out that I prayed. It was not long after that my friend found himself in an anxious frame of mind. He hooked a large trout, which came home on him so suddenly

that he had not time to reel up his line, and in
his extremity he stretched his tall form into the air
and lifted up his pole to an incredible height. He
checked the trout before it got under the boat, but
dared not come down an inch, and then began his
amusing further elongation in reaching for his reel
with one hand, while he carried it ten feet into the
air with the other. A step-ladder would perhaps
have been more welcome to him just then than at
any other moment during his life. But the trout was
saved, though my friend's buttons and suspenders
suffered.

We learned a new trick in fly-fishing here, worth
disclosing. It was not one day in four that the
trout would take the fly on the surface. When
the south wind was blowing and the clouds threatened rain, they would at times, notably about three
o'clock, rise handsomely. But on all other occasions it was rarely that we could entice them up
through the twelve or fifteen feet of water. Earlier
in the season they are not so lazy and indifferent,
but the August languor and drowsiness were now
upon them. So we learned by a lucky accident
to fish deep for them, even weighting our leaders
with a shot, and allowing the flies to sink nearly
to the bottom. After a moment's pause we would
draw them slowly up, and when half or two thirds
of the way to the top the trout would strike, when
the sport became lively enough. Most of our fish

were taken in this way. There is nothing like the flash and the strike at the surface, and perhaps only the need of food will ever tempt the genuine angler into any more prosaic style of fishing; but if you must go below the surface, a shotted leader is the best thing to use.

Our camp-fire at night served more purposes than one; from its embers and flickering shadows, Uncle Nathan read us many a tale of his life in the woods. They were the same old hunter's stories, except that they evidently had the merit of being strictly true, and hence were not very thrilling or marvelous. Uncle Nathan's tendency was rather to tone down and belittle his experiences than to exaggerate them. If he ever bragged at all (and I suspect he did just a little, when telling us how he outshot one of the famous riflemen of the American team, whom he was guiding through these woods), he did it in such a sly, roundabout way that it was hard to catch him at it. His passage with the rifleman referred to shows the difference between the practical offhand skill of the hunter in the woods and the science of the long-range target-hitter. Mr. Bull's Eye had heard that his guide was a capital shot, and had seen some proof of it, and hence could not rest till he had had a trial of skill with him. Uncle Nathan, being the challenged party, had the right to name the distance and the conditions. A piece of white paper the size of a silver dollar was put up on a tree twelve rods off, the contestants to fire three shots each offhand. Uncle Nathan's first bullet barely missed the mark, but the other two were planted well into it. Then the great rifleman took his turn, and missed every time.

"By hemp!" said Uncle Nathan, "I was sorry I shot so well, Mr. —— took it so to heart; and I had used his own rifle, too. He did not get over it for a week."

But far more ignominious was the failure of Mr. Bull's Eye when he saw his first bear. They were paddling slowly and silently down Dead River, when the guide heard a slight noise in the bushes just behind a little bend. He whispered to the rifleman, who sat kneeling in the bow of the boat, to take his rifle. But instead of doing so, he picked up his two-barreled shotgun. As they turned the point, there stood a bear not twenty yards away, drinking from the stream. Uncle Nathan held the canoe, while the man who had come so far in quest of this very game was trying to lay down his shotgun and pick up his rifle. "His hand moved like the hand of a clock," said Uncle Nathan, "and I could hardly keep my seat. I knew the bear would see us in a moment more and run." Instead of laying his gun by his side, where it belonged, he reached it across in front of him, and laid it upon his rifle, and in trying to get the latter from under it a noise was made; the bear heard it and raised his head. Still there was time, for as the bear sprang into the woods he stopped and looked back, — " as I knew he would," said the guide; yet the marksman was not ready. " By hemp! I could have shot three bears," exclaimed Uncle Nathan, " while he was getting that rifle to his face!"

Poor Mr. Bull's Eye was deeply humiliated. " Just the chance I had been looking for," he said, " and my wits suddenly left me."

As a hunter, Uncle Nathan always took the game on its own terms, that of still-hunting. He even shot foxes in this way, going into the fields in the fall just at break of day, and watching for them about their mousing haunts. One morning, by these tactics, he shot a black fox; a fine specimen, he said, and a wild one, for he stopped and looked and listened every few yards.

He had killed over two hundred moose, a large number of them at night on the lakes. His method was to go out in his canoe and conceal himself by some point or island, and wait till he heard the game. In the fall the moose comes into the water to eat the large fibrous roots of the pond-lilies. He splashes along till he finds a suitable spot, when he begins feeding, sometimes thrusting his head and neck several feet under water. The hunter listens, and when the moose lifts his head and the rills of water run from it, and he hears him " swash " the lily roots about to get off the mud, it is his time

to start. Silently as a shadow he creeps up on the
moose, who, by the way, it seems, never suspects
the approach of danger from the water side. If the
hunter accidentally makes a noise, the moose looks
toward the shore for it. There is always a slight
gleam on the water, Uncle Nathan says, even in the
darkest night, and the dusky form of the moose can
be distinctly seen upon it. When the hunter sees
this darker shadow, he lifts his gun to the sky and
gets the range of its barrels, then lowers it till it
covers the mark, and fires.

The largest moose Uncle Nathan ever killed is
mounted in the State House at Augusta. He shot
him while hunting in winter on snow-shoes. The
moose was reposing upon the ground, with his head
stretched out in front of him, as one may sometimes
see a cow resting. The position was such that only
a quartering shot through the animal's hip could
reach its heart. Studying the problem carefully,
and taking his own time, the hunter fired. The
moose sprang into the air, turned, and came with
tremendous strides straight toward him. " I knew
he had not seen or scented me," said Uncle Nathan, " but, by hemp, I wished myself somewhere
else just then; for I was lying right down in his
path." But the noble animal stopped a few yards
short, and fell dead with a bullet hole through his
heart.

When the moose yard in the winter, that is,

restrict their wanderings to a well-defined section of the forest or mountain, trampling down the snow and beating paths in all directions, they browse off only the most dainty morsels first; when they go over the ground a second time they crop a little cleaner; the third time they sort still closer, till by and by nothing is left. Spruce, hemlock, poplar, the barks of various trees, everything within reach, is cropped close. When the hunter comes upon one of these yards, the problem for him to settle is, Where are the moose? for it is absolutely necessary that he keep on the lee side of them. So he considers the lay of the land, the direction of the wind, the time of day, the depth of the snow, examines the spoor, the cropped twigs, and studies every hint and clew like a detective. Uncle Nathan said he could not explain to another how he did it, but he could usually tell in a few minutes in what direction to look for the game. His experience had ripened into a kind of intuition or winged reasoning that was above rules.

He said that most large game, — deer, caribou, moose, bear, — when started by the hunter and not much scared, were sure to stop and look back before disappearing from sight; he usually waited for this last and best chance to fire. He told us of a huge bear he had seen one morning while still-hunting foxes in the fields; the bear saw him, and got into the woods before he could get a good shot. In her course, some distance up the mountain, was a bald, open spot, and he felt sure when she crossed this spot she would pause and look behind her; and sure enough, like Lot's wife, her curiosity got the better of her; she stopped to have a final look, and her travels ended there and then.

Uncle Nathan had trapped and shot a great many bears, and some of his experiences revealed an unusual degree of sagacity in this animal. One April, when the weather began to get warm and thawy, an old bear left her den in the rocks, and built a large, warm nest of grass, leaves, and the bark of the white cedar, under a tall balsam fir that stood in a low, sunny, open place amid the mountains. Hither she conducted her two cubs, and the family began life in what might be called their spring residence. The tree above them was for shelter, and for refuge for the cubs in case danger approached, as it soon did in the form of Uncle Nathan. He happened that way soon after the bear had moved. Seeing her track in the snow, he concluded to follow it. When the bear had passed, the snow had been soft and sploshy, and she had "slumped," he said, several inches. It was now hard and slippery. As he neared the tree, the track turned and doubled, and tacked this way and that, and led through the worst brush and brambles to be found. This was a shrewd thought of the old bear; she could thus hear her enemy coming a long time before he drew very near. When Uncle Nathan finally reached the nest, he found it empty, but still warm. Then he began to circle about and look for the bear's footprints or nailprints upon the frozen snow. Not finding them the first time, he took a larger circle, then a still larger ; finally he made a long dètour, and spent nearly an hour searching for some clew to the direction the bear had taken, but all to no purpose. Then he returned to the tree and scrutinized it. The foliage was very dense, but presently he made out one of the cubs near the top, standing up amid the branches, and peering down at him. This he killed. Further search revealed only a mass of foliage apparently more dense than usual, but a bullet sent into it was followed by loud whimpering and crying, and the other baby bear came tumbling down. In leaving the place, greatly puzzled as to what had become of the mother bear, Uncle Nathan followed another of her frozen tracks, and after about a quarter of a mile saw beside it, upon the snow, the fresh trail he had been in search of. In making her escape, the bear had stepped exactly in her old tracks that were hard and icy, and had thus left no mark till she took to the snow again.

During his trapping expeditions into the woods in midwinter, I was curious to know how Uncle Nathan passed the nights, as we were twice pinched with the cold at that season in our tent and blan-

kets. It was no trouble to keep warm, he said, in
the coldest weather. As night approached, he would
select a place for his camp on the side of a hill.
With one of his snow-shoes he would shovel out the
snow till the ground was reached, carrying the snow
out in front, as we scrape the earth out of the side
of a hill to level up a place for the house and yard.
On this level place, which, however, was made to
incline slightly toward the hill, his bed of boughs
was made. On the ground he had uncovered he
built his fire. His bed was thus on a level with the
fire, and the heat could not thaw the snow under
him and let him down, or the burning logs roll
upon him. With a steep ascent behind it, the fire
burned better, and the wind was not so apt to drive
the smoke and blaze in upon him. Then, with the
long, curving branches of the spruce stuck thickly
around three sides of the bed, and curving over
and uniting their tops above it, a shelter was formed
that would keep out the cold and the snow, and
that would catch and retain the warmth of the
fire. Rolled in his blanket in such a nest, Uncle
Nathan had passed hundreds of the most frigid
winter nights.

One day we made an excursion of three miles
through the woods to Bald Mountain, following a
dim trail. We saw, as we filed silently along, plenty
of signs of caribou, deer, and bear, but were not
blessed with a sight of either of the animals them-

selves. I noticed that Uncle Nathan, in looking through the woods, did not hold his head as we did, but thrust it slightly forward, and peered under the branches like a deer, or other wild creature.

The summit of Bald Mountain was the most impressive mountain-top I had ever seen, mainly, perhaps, because it was one enormous crown of nearly naked granite. The rock had that gray, elemental, eternal look which granite alone has. One seemed to be face to face with the gods of the fore-world. Like an atom, like a breath of to-day, we were suddenly confronted by abysmal geologic time, — the eternities past and the eternities to come. The enormous cleavage of the rocks, the appalling cracks and fissures, the rent boulders, the smitten granite floors, gave one a new sense of the power of heat and frost. In one place we noticed several deep parallel grooves, made by the old glaciers. In the depressions on the summit there was a hard, black, peaty-like soil that looked indescribably ancient and unfamiliar. Out of this mould, which might have come from the moon or the interplanetary spaces, were growing mountain cranberries and blueberries or huckleberries. We were soon so absorbed in gathering the latter that we were quite oblivious of the grandeurs about us. It is these blueberries that attract the bears. In eating them, Uncle Nathan said, they take the bushes in their mouths, and by an upward movement strip them clean both of

leaves and berries. We were constantly on the look-
out for the bears, but failed to see any. Yet a few
days afterward, when two of our party returned
here and encamped upon the mountain, they saw
five during their stay, but failed to get a good shot.
The rifle was in the wrong place each time. The
man with the shotgun saw an old bear and two
cubs lift themselves from behind a rock and twist
their noses around for his scent, and then shrink
away. They were too far off for his buckshot. I
must not forget the superb view that lay before us,
a wilderness of woods and waters stretching away
to the horizon on every hand. Nearly a dozen lakes
and ponds could be seen, and in a clearer atmosphere the foot of Moosehead Lake would have been
visible. The highest and most striking mountain
to be seen was Mount Bigelow, rising above Dead
River, far to the west, and its two sharp peaks
notching the horizon like enormous saw-teeth. We
walked around and viewed curiously a huge boulder
on the top of the mountain that had been split in
two vertically, and one of the halves moved a few
feet out of its bed. It looked recent and familiar,
but suggested gods instead of men. The force that
moved the rock had plainly come from the north.
I thought of a similar boulder I had seen not long
before on the highest point of the Shawangunk
Mountains, in New York, one side of which is
propped up with a large stone, as wall-builders prop

up a rock to wrap a chain around it. The rock seems poised lightly, and has but a few points of bearing. In this instance, too, the power had come from the north.

The prettiest botanical specimen my trip yielded was a little plant that bears the ugly name of horned bladderwort, and which I found growing in marshy places along the shores of Moxie Lake. It has a slender, naked stem nearly a foot high, crowned by two or more large deep yellow flowers, — flowers the shape of little bonnets or hoods. One almost expected to see tiny faces looking out of them. This illusion is heightened by the horn or spur of the flower, which projects from the hood like a long tapering chin, — some masker's device. Then the cape behind, — what a smart upward curve it has, as if spurned by the fairy shoulders it was meant to cover ! But perhaps the most notable thing about the flower was its fragrance, — the richest and strongest perfume I have ever found in a wild flower. This our botanist, Gray, does not mention, as if one should describe the lark and forget its song. The fragrance suggested that of white clover, but was more rank and spicy.

The woods about Moxie Lake were literally carpeted with linnæa. I had never seen it in such profusion. In early summer, the period of its bloom what a charming spectacle the mossy floors of these remote woods must present ! The flowers are pur-

ple rose-color, nodding and fragrant. Another very
abundant plant in these woods was the *Clintonia
borealis*. Uncle Nathan said it was called "bear's
corn," though he did not know why. The only
noticeable flower by the Maine roadsides at this
season that is not common in other parts of the
country is the harebell. Its bright blue, bell-shaped
corolla shone out from amid the dry grass and
weeds all along the route. It was one of the most
delicate roadside flowers I had ever seen.

The only new bird I saw in Maine was the
pileated woodpecker, or black "log-cock," called by
Uncle Nathan "woodcock." I had never before
seen or heard this bird, and its loud cackle in the
woods about Moxie was a new sound to me. It is
the wildest and largest of our northern woodpeckers, and the rarest. Its voice and the sound
of its hammer are heard only in the depths of the
northern woods. It is about as large as a crow,
and nearly as black.

We stayed a week at Moxie, or until we became
surfeited with its trout, and had killed the last
merganser duck that lingered about our end of the
lake. The trout that had accumulated on our
hands we had kept alive in a large champagne
basket submerged in the lake, and the morning
we broke camp the basket was towed to the shore
and opened ; and after we had feasted our eyes
upon the superb spectacle, every trout — there were

twelve or fifteen, some of them two-pounders —
was allowed to swim back into the lake. They
went leisurely, in couples and in trios, and were
soon kicking up their heels in their old haunts. I
expect that the divinity who presides over Moxie
will see to it that every one of those trout, doubled
in weight, comes to our basket in the future.

SPRING JOTTINGS

FOR ten or more years past I have been in the habit of jotting down, among other things in my note-book, observations upon the seasons as they passed, — the complexion of the day, the aspects of nature, the arrival of the birds, the opening of the flowers, or any characteristic feature of the passing moment or hour which the great open-air panorama presented. Some of these notes and observations touching the opening and the progress of the spring season follow herewith.

I need hardly say they are off-hand and informal; what they have to recommend them to the general reader is mainly their fidelity to actual fact. The sun always crosses the line on time, but the seasons which he makes are by no means so punctual; they loiter or they hasten, and the spring tokens are three or four weeks earlier or later some seasons than others. The ice often breaks up on the river early in March, but I have crossed upon it as late as the 10th of April. My journal presents many samples of both early and late springs.

But before I give these extracts, let me say a word

or two in favor of the habit of keeping a journal of
one's thoughts and days. To a countryman, especially of a meditative turn, who likes to preserve the
flavor of the passing moment, or to a person of leisure anywhere, who wants to make the most of life,
a journal will be found a great help. It is a sort
of deposit account wherein one saves up bits and
fragments of his life that would otherwise be lost
to him.

What seemed so insignificant in the passing, or as
it lay in embryo in his mind, becomes a valuable
part of his experiences when it is fully unfolded and
recorded in black and white. The process of writing
develops it; the bud becomes the leaf or flower;
the one is disentangled from the many and takes
definite form and hue. I remember that Thoreau
says in a letter to a friend, after his return from a
climb to the top of Monadnock, that it is not till he
gets home that he really goes over the mountain;
that is, I suppose, sees what the climb meant to
him when he comes to write an account of it to his
friend. Every one's experience is probably much
the same; when we try to tell what we saw and felt,
even to our journals, we discover more and deeper
meanings in things than we had suspected.

The pleasure and value of every walk or journey
we take may be doubled to us by carefully noting
down the impressions it makes upon us. How much
of the flavor of Maine birch I should have missed

had I not compelled that vague, unconscious being within me, who absorbs so much and says so little, to unbosom himself at the point of the pen! It was not till after I got home that I really went to Maine, or to the Adirondacks, or to Canada. Out of the chaotic and nebulous impressions which these expeditions gave me, I evolved the real experience. There is hardly anything that does not become much more in the telling than in the thinking or in the feeling.

I see the fishermen floating up and down the river above their nets, which are suspended far out of sight in the water beneath them. They do not know what fish they have got, if any, till after a while they lift the nets up and examine them. In all of us there is a region of subconsciousness above which our ostensible lives go forward, and in which much comes to us, or is slowly developed, of which we are quite ignorant until we lift up our nets and inspect them.

Then the charm and significance of a day are so subtle and fleeting! Before we know it, it is gone past all recovery. I find that each spring, that each summer and fall and winter of my life, has a hue and quality of its own, given by some prevailing mood, a train of thought, an event, an experience, — a color or quality of which I am quite unconscious at the time, being too near to it, and too completely enveloped by it. But afterward some mood or cir-

cumstance, an odor, or fragment of a tune, brings
it back as by a flash; for one brief second the
adamantine door of the past swings open and gives
me a glimpse of my former life. One's journal,
dashed off without any secondary motive, may often
preserve and renew the past for him in this way.

These leaves from my own journal are not very
good samples of this sort of thing, but they preserve
for me the image of many a day which memory alone
could never have kept.

March 3, 1879. The sun is getting strong, but
winter still holds his own. No hint of spring in the
earth or air. No sparrow or sparrow song yet. But
on the 5th there was a hint of spring. The day
warm and the snow melting. The first bluebird
note this morning. How sweetly it dropped down
from the blue overhead!

March 10. A real spring day at last, and a rouser!
Thermometer between fifty and sixty degrees in the
coolest spot; bees very lively about the hive, and
working on the sawdust in the wood-yard; how they
dig and wallow in the woody meal, apparently
squeezing it, as if forcing it to yield up something to
them! Here they get their first substitute for pollen. The sawdust of hickory and maple is preferred.
The inner milky substance between the bark and
the wood, called the cambium layer, is probably the
source of their supplies.

In the growing tree it is in this layer or secretion

that the vital processes are the most active and potent. It has been found by experiment that this tender, milky substance is capable of exerting a very great force; a growing tree exerts a lifting and pushing force of more than thirty pounds to the square inch, and the force is thought to reside in the soft, fragile cells that make up the cambium layer. It is like the strength of Samson residing in his hair. Saw one bee enter the hive with pollen on his back, which he must have got from some open greenhouse; or had he found the skunk cabbage in bloom ahead of me?

The bluebirds! It seemed as if they must have been waiting somewhere close by for the first warm day, like actors behind the scenes, for they were here in numbers early in the morning; they rushed upon the stage very promptly when their parts were called. No robins yet. Sap runs, but not briskly. It is too warm and still; it wants a brisk day for sap, with a certain sharpness in the air, a certain crispness and tension.

March 12. A change to more crispness and coolness, but a delicious spring morning. Hundreds of snowbirds with a sprinkling of song and Canada sparrows are all about the house, chirping and lisping and chattering in a very animated manner. The air is full of bird voices; through this maze of fine sounds comes the strong note and warble of the robin, and the soft call of the bluebird. A few days ago, not a bird, not a sound; everything rigid and severe; then in a day the barriers of winter give way, and spring comes like an inundation. In a twinkling all is changed.

Under date of February 27, 1881, I find this note: "Warm; saw the male bluebird warbling and calling cheerily. The male bluebird spreads his tail as he flits about at this season, in a way to make him look very gay and dressy. It adds to his expression considerably, and makes him look alert and beau-like, and every inch a male. The grass is green under the snow, and has grown perceptibly. The warmth of the air seems to go readily through a covering of ice and snow. Note how quickly the ice lets go of the door-stones, though completely covered, when the day becomes warm."

The farmers say a deep snow draws the frost out of the ground. It is certain that the frost goes out when the ground is deeply covered for some time, though it is of course the warmth rising up from the depths of the ground that does it. A winter of deep snows is apt to prove fatal to the peach buds. The frost leaves the ground, the soil often becomes so warm that angle-worms rise to near the surface, the sap in the trees probably stirs a little; then there comes a cold wave, the mercury goes down to ten or fifteen below zero, and the peach buds are killed. It is not the cold alone that does it; it is the warmth at one end and the extreme cold at the other. When the snow is removed so that the frost can get at the roots also, peach buds will stand fourteen or fifteen degrees below zero.

March 7, 1881. A perfect spring day at last, — still, warm, and without a cloud. Tapped two trees; the sap runs, the snow runs, everything runs. Blue-birds the only birds yet. Thermometer forty-two degrees in the shade. A perfect sap day. A perfect sap day is a crystalline day; the night must have a keen edge of frost, and the day a keen edge of air and sun, with wind north or northwest. The least film, the least breath from the south, the least sug-gestion of growth, and the day is marred as a sap day. Maple sap is maple frost melted by the sun. (9 P. M.) A soft, large-starred night; the moon in her second quarter; perfectly still and freezing; Venus throbbing low in the west. A crystalline night.

March 21, 1884. The top of a high barometric wave, a day like a crest, lifted up, sightly, sparkling. A cold snap without storm issuing in this clear, daz-zling, sharp, northern day. How light, as if illu-minated by more than the sun; the sky is full of light; light seems to be streaming up all around the horizon. The leafless trees make no shadows; the woods are flooded with light; everything shines; a day large and imposing, breathing strong masculine breaths out of the north; a day without a speck or film, winnowed through and through, all the win-dows and doors of the sky open. Day of crumpled rivers and lakes, of crested waves, of bellying sails, high-domed and lustrous day. The only typical March day of the bright heroic sort we have yet had.

March 24, 1884. Damp, still morning, much fog on the river. All the branches and twigs of the trees strung with drops of water. The grass and weeds beaded with fog drops. Two lines of ducks go up the river, one a few feet beneath the other. On second glance the under line proves to be the reflection of the other in the still water. As the ducks cross a large field of ice, the lower line is suddenly blotted out, as if the birds had dived beneath the ice. A train of cars across the river, — the train sunk beneath a solid stratum of fog, its plume of smoke and vapor unrolling above it and slanting away in the distance; a liquid morning; the turf buzzes as you walk over it.

Skunk cabbage on Saturday the 22d, probably in bloom several days. This plant always gets ahead of me. It seems to come up like a mushroom in a single night. Water newts just out, and probably piping before the frogs, though not certain about this.

March 25. One of the rare days that go before a storm; the flower of a series of days increasingly fair. To-morrow, probably, the flower falls, and days of rain and cold prepare the way for another fair day or days. The barometer must be high to-day; the birds fly high. I feed my bees on a rock, and sit long and watch them covering the combs, and rejoice in the multitudinous humming. The river is a great mirror dotted here and there by small cakes of ice. The first sloop comes lazily on up the flood tide, like the first butterfly of spring; the little steamer, our river omnibus, makes her first trip, and wakes the echoes with her salutatory whistle, her flags dancing in the sun.

April 1. Welcome to April, my natal month; the month of the swelling buds, the springing grass, the first nests, the first plantings, the first flowers, and, last but not least, the first shad! The door of the seasons first stands ajar this month, and gives us a peep beyond. The month in which to begin the world, in which to begin your house, in which to begin your courtship, in which to enter upon any new enterprise. The bees usually get their first pollen this month and their first honey. All hibernating creatures are out before April is past. The coon, the chipmunk, the bear, the turtles, the frogs, the snakes, come forth beneath April skies.

April 8. A day of great brightness and clearness, — a crystalline April day that precedes snow. In this sharp crisp air the flakes are forming. As in a warm streaming south wind one can almost smell the swelling buds, so a wind from the opposite quarter at this season as often suggests the crystalline snow. I go up in the sugar bush [this was up among the Catskills], and linger for an hour among the old trees. The air is still, and has the property of being "hollow," as the farmers say; that is, it is heavy, motionless, and transmits sounds well. Every warble of a bluebird or robin, or caw of crow, or bark of dog, or bleat of sheep, or cackle of geese, or call of boy or man, within the landscape, comes distinctly to the ear. The smoke from the chimney goes straight up.

I walk through the bare fields; the shore larks run or flit before me; I hear their shuffling, gurgling, lisping, half-inarticulate song. Only of late years have I noticed the shore larks in this section. Now they breed and pass the summer on these hills, and I am told that they are gradually becoming permanent residents in other parts of the State. They are nearly as large as the English skylark, with conspicuous black markings about the head and throat; shy birds squatting in the sere grass, and probably taken by most country people who see them to be sparrows.

Their flight and manner in song is much like that of the skylark. The bird mounts up and up on ecstatic wing, till it becomes a mere speck against the sky, where it drifts to and fro, and utters at intervals its crude song, a mere fraction or rudiment of the skylark's song, a few sharp, lisping, unmelodious notes, as if the bird had a bad cold, and could only now and then make any sound, — heard a long distance, but insignificant, a mere germ of the true lark's song; as it were the first rude attempt of na-- ture in this direction. After due trial and waiting, it develops the lark's song itself. But if the law of evolution applies to bird-songs as well as to other things, the shore lark should in time become a fine songster. I know of no bird-song that seems so obviously struggling to free itself and reach a fuller expression. As the bird seems more and more in- clined to abide permanently amid cultivated fields, and to forsake the wild and savage north, let us hope that its song is also undergoing a favorable change.

How conspicuous the crows in the brown fields, or against the lingering snow-banks, or in the clear sky! How still the air! One could carry a lighted candle over the hills. The light is very strong, and the effect of the wall of white mountains rising up all around from the checkered landscape, and holding up the blue dome of the sky, is strange indeed.

April 14. A delicious day, warm as May. This to me is the most bewitching part of the whole year. One's relish is so keen, and the morsels are so few and so tender. How the fields of winter rye stand out! They call up visions of England. A perfect day in April far excels a perfect day in June, because it provokes and stimulates while the latter sates and cloys. Such days have all the peace and geniality of summer without any of its satiety or enervating heat.

April 15. Not much cloud this morning, but much vapor in the air. A cool south wind with streaks of a pungent vegetable odor, probably from the willows. When I make too dead a set at it, I miss it; but when I let my nose have its own way, and take in the air slowly, I get it, an odor as of a myriad swelling buds. The long-drawn call of the high-hole comes up from the fields, then the tender rapid trill of the bush or russet sparrow, then the piercing note of the meadowlark, a flying shaft of sound.

April 21. The enchanting days continue without a break. One's senses are not large enough to take them all in. Maple buds just bursting, apple-trees full of infantile leaves. How the poplars and willows stand out! A moist, warm, brooding haze over all the earth. All day my little russet sparrow sings and trills divinely. The most prominent bird music in April is from the sparrows.

The yellowbirds (goldfinches) are just getting on their yellow coats. I saw some yesterday that had a smutty, unwashed look, because of the new yellow shining through the old drab-colored webs of the feathers. These birds do not shed their feathers in the spring, as careless observers are apt to think they do, but merely shed the outer webs of their feathers and quills, which peel off like a glove from the hand.

All the groves and woods lightly touched with new foliage. Looks like May; violets and dandelions in bloom. Sparrow's nest with two eggs. Maples hanging out their delicate fringe-like bloom. First barn swallows may be looked for any day after April 20.

This period may be called the vernal equipoise, and corresponds to the October calm called the Indian summer.

April 2, 1890. The second of the April days, clear as a bell. The eye of the heavens wide open at last. A sparrow day; how they sang! And the robins, too, before I was up in the morning. Now and then I could hear the rat-tat-tat of the downy at his drum. How many times I paused at my work to drink in the beauty of the day!

How I like to walk out after supper these days! I stroll over the lawn and stand on the brink of the hill. The sun is down, the robins pipe and call, and as the dusk comes on, they indulge in that loud chiding note or scream, whether in anger or in fun I never can tell. Up the road in the distance the multitudinous voice of the little peepers, — a thicket or screen of sound. An April twilight is unlike any other.

April 12. Lovely, bright day. We plow the ground under the hill for the new vineyard. In opening the furrow for the young vines I guide the team by walking in their front. How I soaked up the sunshine to-day! At night I glowed all over; my whole being had had an earth-bath; such a feeling of freshly plowed land in every cell of my brain. The furrow had struck in; the sunshine had photographed it upon my soul.

April 13. A warm, even hot April day. The air full of haze; the sunshine golden. In the afternoon J. and I walk out over the country north of town. Everybody is out, all the paths and byways are full of boys and young fellows. We sit on a wall a long time by a meadow and an orchard, and drink in the scene. April to perfection, such a sentiment of spring everywhere. The sky is partly overcast, the air moist, just enough so to bring out the odors, — a sweet perfume of bursting, growing things. One could almost eat the turf like a horse. All about the robins sang. In the trees the crow blackbird cackled and jingled. Athwart these sounds came every half minute the clear, strong note of the meadowlark. The larks were very numerous and were lovemaking. Then the high-hole called and the bush sparrow trilled. Arbutus days these, everybody wants to go to the woods for arbutus; it fairly calls one. The soil calls for the plow, too, the garden calls for the spade, the vineyard calls for the hoe. From all about the farm voices call, Come and do this, or do that. At night, how the " peepers " pile up the sound!

How I delight to see the plow at work such mornings! the earth is ripe for it, fairly lusts for it, and the freshly turned soil looks good enough to eat.

Plucked my first blood-root this morning, — a full blown flower with a young one folded up in a leaf beneath it, only the bud emerging, like the head of a pappoose protruding from its mother's blanket, — a very pretty sight. The blood-root always comes up with the leaf shielding the flower-bud, as one shields the flame of the candle in the open air with his hand half closed about it.

These days the song of the toad — *tr-r-r-r-r-r-r-r-r-r-r-r-r-r-r-r-r-r-r* — is heard in the land. At nearly all hours I hear it, and it is as welcome to me as the song of any bird. It is a kind of gossamer of sound drifting in the air. Mother toad is in the pools and puddles now depositing that long chain or raveling of eggs, while her dapper little mate rides upon her back and fertilizes them as they are laid. As I look toward the fields where the first brown thrasher is singing, I see emerald patches of rye. The unctuous, confident strain of the bird seems to make the fields grow greener hour by hour.

May 4. The perfection of early May weather. How green the grass, how happy the birds, how placid the river, how busy the bees, how soft the air! — that kind of weather when there seems to be dew in the air all day, — the day a kind of prolonged morning, — so fresh, so wooing, so caressing! The baby leaves on the apple-trees have doubled in size since last night.

March 12, 1891. Had positive proof this morning that at least one song sparrow has come back to his haunts of a year ago. One year ago to-day my attention was attracted, while walking over to the post-office, by an unfamiliar bird-song. It caught my ear while I was a long way off. I followed it up and found that it proceeded from a song sparrow. Its chief feature was one long, clear high note, very strong, sweet, and plaintive. It sprang out of the trills and quavers of the first part of the bird-song, like a long arc or parabola of sound. To my mental vision it rose far up against the blue, and turned sharply downward again and finished in more trills and quavers. I had never before heard anything like it. It was the usual long, silvery note in the sparrow's song greatly increased; indeed, the whole breath and force of the bird were put in this note, so that you caught little else than this silver loop of sound. The bird remained in one locality — the bushy corner of a field — the whole season. He indulged in the ordinary sparrow song, also. I had repeatedly had my eye upon him when he changed from one to the other.

And now here he is again, just a year after, in the same place, singing the same remarkable song, capturing my ear with the same exquisite lasso of sound. What would I not give to know just where he passed the winter, and what adventures by flood and field befell him!

(I will add that the bird continued in song the

whole season, apparently confining his wanderings to a few acres of ground. But the following spring he did not return, and I have never heard him since, and if any of his progeny inherited this peculiar song, I have not heard them.)

IN YAKUTAT BAY

After four warm, humid days at Sitka we turned our faces for the first time toward the open ocean, our objective point being Yakutat Bay, a day's run farther north. The usual Alaska excursion ends at Sitka, but ours was now only fairly begun. The Pacific was very good to us, and used us as gently as an inland lake, there being only a long, low, sleepy swell that did not disturb the most sensitive. The next day, Sunday the 18th, was mild and placid. Far at sea on our left we looked into a world of sunshine, but above us and on our right lay a heavy blanket of clouds, enveloping and blotting out all the upper portions of the great Fairweather Range. We steamed all day a few miles offshore, hoping that the great peaks, some of them fifteen thousand to sixteen thousand feet high, would reveal themselves, but they did not. We saw them only from the waist down, as it were, with their glaciers like vast white aprons flanked by skirts of spruce forests.

One of these glaciers, La Perouse, came quite down
to the sea, with a front a mile or more long and two
hundred feet high. At one point it had cut into the
edge of the forest, and shoved and piled up the trees
and soil as a heavy vehicle shoves and folds up the
turf. This, of course, showed that quite recently
the glacier had had a period of advance or augmen-
tation, and had encroached upon its banks. We
stopped an hour in front of it and put a party ashore,
but they learned little that could not be divined
from the ship. They found a heavy surf running,
and did not get through it on their return without an
acquaintance with the Pacific more intimate than
agreeable. All day long we were in sight of glaciers,
usually two or three at a time, some of them immense, all the offspring of the great Fairweather
Range. Now and then the back of one some miles
inland would show above a low wooded ridge, a line
of white above an expanse of black, like the crest of
a river about to overflow its banks. One broad ice
slope I recall which, with its dark, straight lines of
moraine dividing it into three equal portions, suggested a side-hill farm in winter with the tops of the
stone walls showing above the snow. It had a
friendly, home look to me.

On the morning of the 19th we were at anchor
in front of the Indian village in Yakutat Bay. This
bay is literally like an arm, a huge arm of the sea,
very broad and heavy at the shoulder, much flexed

at the elbow, where it breaks into the St. Elias
Range, and long and slender in the forearm, which
is thrust through the mountains till it nearly reaches
the sea again. Eight or ten comfortable frame
houses, with a store and post-office, made up the
Indian village known on the map as Yakutat. It sat
low on a wooded point just to one side of the broad
entrance to the bay. There were upwards of a hundred people there, looked after by a Swedish mis-
sionary. We soon proceeded up the bay, with the
great Malaspina Glacier on our left, and put off
three hunting and collecting parties, to be absent
from the ship till Thursday. The event of this day
was the view of Mt. St. Elias that was vouchsafed
us for half an hour in the afternoon. The base and
lower ranges had been visible for some time, bathed
in clear sunshine, but a heavy canopy of dun-colored
clouds hung above us, and stretched away toward
the mountain, dropping down there in many cur-
tain-like folds, hiding the peak. But the scene-
shifters were at work; slowly the heavy folds of
clouds that limited our view yielded and were spun
off by the air currents, till at last the veil was completely rent, and there, in the depths of clear air and
sunshine, the huge mass soared to heaven.

There is sublimity in the sight of a summer
thunder-head with its great white and dun convolu-
tions rising up for miles against the sky, but there is
more in the vision of a jagged mountain crest pier-

cing the blue at even a lesser height. This is partly because it is a much rarer spectacle, but mainly because it is a display of power that takes greater hold of the imagination. That lift heavenward of the solid crust of the earth, that aspiration of the insensate rocks, that effort of the whole range, as it were, to carry one peak into heights where all may not go, — every lower summit seeming to second it and shoulder it forward till it stands there in a kind of serene astronomic solitude and remoteness, — is a vision that always shakes the heart of the beholder.

Later in the day we continued our course up the bay through much drift ice, and were soon in sight of two large glaciers, the Turner and the Hubbard. Both presented long, high palisades of ice to the water, like the Muir, but were far less active and explosive. The Hubbard Glacier is just at the sharp bend of the elbow, a regular "fiddler's" elbow, where the bay, much narrowed, turns abruptly from northeast to south. Here, with a Yakutat Indian for pilot, we entered upon the strange and weird scenery of Russell Fiord, and into waters that no ship as large as ours had before navigated. This part of the bay is in size like the Hudson and about sixty miles in length, but how wild and savage! A succession of mountains of almost naked rock, now scored and scalloped and polished by the old glaciers, now with vast moraines upon their sides or heaped at their

feet, which the rains and melting snows have plowed
and ribbed and carved into many fantastic forms.
There was an air of seclusion and remoteness about
it all, as if this had been a special playground of the
early ice gods, a nook or alley set apart for them in
which to indulge every whim and fancy. And what
could be more whimsical or fantastic than yonder
glacier playing the mountain goat, clinging to the
steep sides of the mountain or breaking over its
cliffs and yet falling not, hanging there like a congealed torrent, a silent and motionless shadow. The
eye seems baffled. Surely the ice is plunging or will
plunge the next second: but no, there it is fixed; it
bends over the brink, it foams below, but no sound
is heard and no movement is apparent. You see the
corrugated surface where it emerges from its great
snow reservoir on the mountain summit; it shows
deep crevasses where it sweeps down a steep incline,
then curves across a terrace, then leaps in solid,
fixed foam down the face of the cliff, to which it
seems bound as by some magic.

These precipice glaciers apparently move no faster
than those in the valley. It is in all cases a subtle,
invisible movement, like that of the astronomic
bodies. It would seem as if gravity had little to do
with it. They do not gain momentum like an ava-
lanche of snow or earth, but creep so slowly that to
the lookers-on they are as motionless as the rocks
themselves. The grade, the obstacles in the way,

seem to make no difference. One would think that if a mass of ice, weighing many thousand tons, hanging upon the face of a mountain-wall steeper than a house roof, detached itself from the rest at all and began to move, it would gain momentum and presently shoot down, as the loosened ice and snow do from our slate roofs. But it does not. If the temperature of the rocks were suddenly raised as in the case of the roof, no doubt the glacier would shoot, but it is not. The under surface of the ice is probably perpetually congealed and perpetually loosened, and the crystallization is constantly broken and constantly reformed, so that the glacier's motion is more a creeping than a sliding. The carving and sculpturing of the rocks is of course done by the pebbles and boulders beneath the ice, and these must slide or roll.

We followed the bay or inlet to its head, and anchored for the night in the large oval that marks its termination. We were about fifteen miles from the Pacific, being separated from it by a low, level moraine of the old glaciers. We were now surrounded by low wooded shores, from which in the long twilight came the sweet vespers of the little hermit thrush.

On the 20th another hunting party went out from the ship, and with an Indian guide climbed and threaded the snow-covered mountains nearly all day in quest of bears, but came back as empty

handed as it had set out. The ship in the mean
time steamed back ten miles to a side arm of the bay,
at the head of which is Hidden Glacier, so called
because hidden from view behind a shoulder of the
mountain. A broad gravel-bed with a stream winding through it, which the retreating glacier had
uncovered, was alone visible from the ship. While
Gannett and Gilbert proceeded to survey and map
the glacier, many of us wandered on shore amid
a world of moraines and gravel-banks. In the afternoon we moved to the vicinity of the Hubbard Glacier, where the ship took a fresh supply of water
from a mountain torrent, while the glacier hunters
viewed the Nunatak Glacier, and the mineralogists
with their hammers prowled upon the shore. My
own diversion that afternoon was to climb one of
the near mountains to an altitude of about twenty-
five hundred feet, where I looked down at a fearful
angle into the sea, and where I found my first tit-
lark's nest. The bird with her shining eyes looked
out upon me, and upon the sublime scene, from a
little cavity in a mossy bank near the snow-line. Her
nest held six dark-brown eggs. Some pussy willows
near by were just starting. I thought to reach the
peak of the mountain up a broad and very steep
band of snow, but I looked back once too often. The
descent to the sea was too easy and too fearful for
my imagination, so I cautiously turned back. In a
large patch of alders at the foot of the mountain four

or five species of birds were nesting and in song. The most welcome sight to me was a solitary barn swallow skimming along as one might have seen it at home, — no barns within hundreds of miles, yet the little swallow seemed quite at her ease.

While we were anchored here, we had another brief vision of surpassing mountain grandeur. The fair weather divinities brushed aside the veil of clouds, and one of the lofty peaks to the north, probably Vancouver, stood revealed to us. We yielded to its mighty spell for a few moments, and then the cloud curtain again dropped.

The next day we left Russell Fiord, and anchored before an Indian encampment below Haenke Island, on the south side of the head of Yakutat Bay. The Indians had come up from their village below, — some of them, we were told, from as far away as Sitka. They were living here in tents and bark huts, and hunting the hair seal amid the drifting icebergs that the Turner and the Hubbard cast off. This was their summer camp; they were laying in a supply of skins and oil against their winter needs. In July they go to the salmon streams and secure their stores of salmon. During these excursions their village at Yakutat is nearly deserted. The encampment we visited was upon the beach of a broad, gravelly delta flanked by high mountains. It was redolent of seal oil. The dead carcasses of the seals lay in rows upon the pebbles in front of the tents and huts. The women and girls were skinning them, and cutting out the blubber and trying it out in pots over smouldering fires, while the crack of the men's shotguns could be heard out amid the ice. Apparently their only food at such times is seal meat, with parts of the leaf or stalk of a kind of cowparsnip, a coarse, rank plant that grows all about. The Indian women frowned upon our photographers, and were very averse to having the cameras pointed at them. It took a good deal of watching and waiting and manœuvring to get a good shot. The artists, with their brushes and canvases, were regarded with less suspicion.

The state of vegetation in Yakutat Bay was like that of early May in New York, though the temperature was lower. Far up the mountain-side near the line of snow the willows were just pushing out. At their base the columbine, rock-loving as at home, but larger and coarser-flowered, was in bloom, and blue violets could be gathered by the handful. Back of the encampment were acres of lupine just bursting into flower. It gave a gay, festive look to the place. Red-vested bumble-bees were working eagerly upon it. The yellow warbler was nesting in the alders near by. New birds added to our list from these shores were the pine grosbeak, the Arctic tern, and the robber jaeger. No large game was secured by our hunters in Yakutat Bay, though Captain Kelly declared he was at one time so near a bear that he could smell him. The bear undoubtedly got a smell of the captain first.

Our party had now been a month together, and had assumed the features of a large and happy family on a summer holiday cruise. We were of diverse interests and types of character, yet one in the spirit of true comradeship. This fortunate condition was due largely to the truly democratic and manly character of the head of the expedition, Mr. Harriman, and to the cheerful and obliging temper of Captain Doran. The pleasure of the party was the pleasure of our host and of the captain. The ship was equally at the service of men who wanted to catch mice or collect a new bird, and of those who wanted to survey a glacier or inlet or to shoot a bear. One day it made a voyage of sixty miles to enable our collectors to take up some traps, the total catch of which proved to be nine mice. The next day it was as likely to go as far to enable Ritter and Saunders to dredge for new forms of sea life, or Devereux to inspect some outcropping of copper ore. Early in the voyage our committee on entertainment arranged a course of lectures. Nearly every night at eight o'clock, on the upper deck or in the Social Hall, some one of our college professors or government specialists held forth. One night it was Dall upon the history or geography of Alaska; then Gilbert upon the agency of glaciers in shaping the valleys and mountains, or upon the glaciers we had recently visited; then Brewer upon climate and ocean currents, or Coville upon some botanical features of the regions about us, or Ritter upon the shore forms of sea life, or Emerson upon volcanoes and lava beds, or John Muir on his experiences upon the glaciers and his adventure with his dog Stikeen in crossing a huge crevasse on a sliver of ice, or Charles Keeler on the coloration of birds, or Fuertes on bird-songs, or Grinnell on Indian tribes and Indian characteristics, and so on. On Sunday evenings Dr. Nelson conducted the Episcopal service and preached a sermon, while at other times books and music and games added to the attraction of the Social Hall.

AUGUST DAYS

ONE of our well-known poets, in personifying August, represents her as coming with daisies in her hair. But an August daisy is a sorry affair; it is little more than an empty, or partly empty, seed-vessel. In the Northern States the daisy is in her girlhood and maidenhood in June; she becomes very matronly early in July, — fat, faded, prosaic, — and by or before August she is practically defunct. I recall no flower whose career is more typical of the life, say, of the average European peasant woman, or of the women of barbarous tribes, its grace and youthfulness pass so quickly into stoutness, obesity, and withered old age. How positively girlish and taking is the daisy during the first few days of its blooming, while its snow-white rays yet stand straight up and shield its tender centre somewhat as a hood shields a girl's face! Presently it becomes a perfect disk and bares its face to the sun; this is the stage of its young womanhood. Then its yellow centre — its body — begins to swell and become gross, the rays slowly turn brown, and finally wither up and drop. It is a flower no longer, but a receptacle packed with ripening seeds.

A relative of the daisy, the orange-colored hawk-weed (*Hieracium aurantiacum*), which within the past twenty years has spread far and wide over New York and New England, is often at the height of its beauty in August, when its deep vivid orange is a delight to the eye. It repeats in our meadows and upon our hilltops the flame of the columbine of May, intensified. The personified August with these flowers in her hair would challenge our admiration and not our criticism. Unlike the daisy, it quickly sprouts again when cut down with the grass in the meadows, and renews its bloom. Parts of New England, at least, have a native August flower quite as brilliant as the hawkweed just described, and far less a usurper; I refer to meadow-beauty, or rhexia, found near the coast, which suggests a purple evening primrose.

Nature has, for the most part, lost her delicate tints in August. She is tanned, hirsute, freckled, like one long exposed to the sun. Her touch is strong and vivid. The coarser, commoner wayside flowers now appear, — vervain, eupatorium, mimulus, the various mints, asters, golden-rod, thistles, fireweed, mulleins, motherwort, catnip, blueweed, turtle-head, sunflowers, clematis, evening primrose, lobelia, gerardia, and, in the marshes of the lower Hudson, marshmallows, and vast masses of the purple loosestrife. Mass and intensity take the place of delicacy and furtiveness. The spirit of Nature has grown bold and aggressive; it is rank and coarse; she flaunts her weeds in our faces. She wears a thistle on her bosom. But I must not forget the delicate rose gerardia, which she also wears upon her bosom, and which suggests that, before the season closes, Nature is getting her hand ready for her delicate spring flora. With me this gerardia lines open paths over dry knolls in the woods, and its little purple bells and smooth, slender leaves form one of the most exquisite tangles of flowers and foliage of the whole summer. It is August matching the color and delicacy of form of the fringed polygala of May. I know a half-wild field bordering a wood, which is red with strawberries in June and pink with gerardia in August.

One may still gather the matchless white pond-lily in this month, though this flower is in the height of its glory earlier in the season, except in the northern lakes.

A very delicate and beautiful marsh flower that may be found on the borders of lakes in northern New York and New England is the horned bladderwort,—yellow, fragrant, and striking in form, like a miniature old-fashioned bonnet, when bonnets covered the head and projected beyond the face, instead of hovering doubtfully above the scalp. The horn curves down and out like a long chin from a face hid-

den within the bonnet. I have found this rare flower
in the Adirondacks and in Maine. It may doubtless
be found in Canada, and in Michigan and Wis-
consin. Britton and Brown say "south to Florida
and Texas." It is the most fragrant August flower
known to me. This month has not many fragrant
flowers to boast of. Besides the above and the pond-
lily I recall two others, — the small purple fringed-
orchis and a species of lady's-tresses (*Spiranthes
cernua*).

The characteristic odors of August are from fruit
— grapes, peaches, apples, pears, melons — and the
ripening grain; yes, and the blooming buckwheat.
Of all the crop and farm odors this last is the most
pronounced and honeyed, rivaling that of the flower-
ing locust of May and of the linden in July.

The mistakes of our lesser poets in dealing with
nature themes might furnish me with many a text in
this connection. Thus one of them makes the call of
the phœbe-bird prominent in August. One would
infer from the poem that the phœbe was not heard
during any other month. Now it is possible that
the poet heard the phœbe in August, but if so, the
occurrence was exceptional, and it is more proba-
ble that it was the wood pewee that he heard. The
phœbe is most noticeable in April and early May,
and its characteristic call is not often heard till the
sun is well up in the sky. Most of our song-birds
are silent in August, or sing only fitfully, as do the

song sparrow and the oriole. The real August songster, and the bird that one comes to associate with
the slow, drowsy days, is the indigo-bird. After
midsummer its song, delivered from the top of some
small tree in the pasture or a bushy field, falls upon
the ear with a peculiar languid, midsummery effect.
The boys and girls gathering raspberries and blackberries hear it; the stroller through the upland fields,
or lounger in the shade of maple or linden, probably
hears no bird-song but this, if he even distinguishes
this from the more strident insect voices. The plumage of the bird is more or less faded by this time,
the vivid indigo of early June is lightly brushed with
a dull sooty shade, but the song is nearly as full as
the earlier strain, and in the dearth of bird voices is
even more noticeable. I do not now recall that any
of our poets have embalmed this little cerulean songster in their verse.

One may also occasionally hear the red-eyed vireo
in August, but it is low tide with him too. His song
has a reminiscent air, like that of the indigo. The
whip-poor-will calls fitfully in this month, and may
be heard even in September; but he quickly checks
himself, as if he knew it was out of season. In the
Adirondacks I have heard the speckled Canada
warbler in August, and the white-throated sparrow.
But nearly all the migratory birds begin to get rest-
less during this month. They cut loose from their
nesting-haunts and drift through the woods in pro-

miscuous bands, and many of them start on their southern journey. From my woods along the Hudson the warblers all disappear before the middle of the month. Some of them are probably in hiding during the moulting season. The orioles begin to move south about the middle of the month, and by the first of September the last of them have passed. They occasionally sing in a suppressed tone during this migration, probably the young males trying their instruments. It is at this time, when full of frolic and mischief, like any other emigrants with faces set to new lands, that they make such havoc in the Hudson River vineyards. They seem to puncture the grapes in the spirit of pure wantonness, or as if on a wager as to who can puncture the most. The swallows — the cliff and the barn — all leave in August, usually by the 20th, though the swift may be seen as late as October. I notice that our poets often detain the swallows much beyond the proper date. One makes them perch upon the barn in October. Another makes them noisy about the eaves in Indian summer. An English poet makes the swallow go at November's bidding. The tree swallow may often be seen migrating in countless numbers along the coast in early October, but long ere this date the barn and the cliff swallows are in tropical climes. They begin to flock, and apparently rehearse the migrating programme, in July.

The bobolinks go in early August with the red-

shouldered starlings, and along the Potomac and
Chesapeake Bay become the reed-birds of sportsmen. One often hears them in this month calling
from high in the air as they journey southward from
more northern latitudes.

About the most noticeable bird of August in New
York and New England is the yellowbird, or goldfinch. This is one of the last birds to nest, seldom
hatching its eggs till late in July. It seems as if a
particular kind of food were required to rear its
brood, which cannot be had at an earlier date. The
seed of the common thistle is apparently its main-
stay. There is no prettier sight at this season than
a troop of young goldfinches, led by their parents,
going from thistle to thistle along the roadside and
pecking the ripe heads to pieces for the seed. The
plaintive call of the young is one of the characteristic August sounds. Their nests are frequently
destroyed, or the eggs thrown from them, by the
terrific July thunder-showers. Last season a pair
had a nest on the slender branch of a maple in front
of the door of the house where I was staying. The
eggs were being deposited, and the happy pair had
many a loving conversation about them many times
each day, when one afternoon a very violent storm
arose which made the branches of the trees stream
out like wildly disheveled hair, quite turning over
those on the windward side, and emptying the pretty
nest of its eggs. In such cases the birds build anew,

— a delay that may bring the incubation into August. Such an accident had probably befallen a pair of which I one season made this ncte in my note-book, under date of August 6: —

" A goldfinches' nest in the maple-tree near the window where I write, the female sitting on four pale bluish-white eggs ; the male feeds her on the nest ; whenever she hears his voice she calls incessantly, much after the manner of the young birds, — the only case I recall of the sitting bird calling while in the act of incubation. The male evidently brings the food in his crop, or at least well back in his beak or throat, as it takes him several moments to deliver it to his mate, which he does by separate morsels. The male, when disturbed by a rival, utters the same note as he pursues his enemy from point to point that the female does when calling to him. It does not sound like a note of anger, but of love and confidence."

As the bird-songs fail, the insect harpers and fiddlers begin. August is the heyday of these musicians. The katydid begins to " work her chromatic reed " early in the month, and with her comes that pulsing, purring monotone of the little pale tree-crickets. These last fill the August twilight with a soft, rhythmic undertone of sound, which forms a sort of background for the loud, strident notes of the katydids.

August, too, is the month of the screaming, high-

sailing hawks. The young are now fully fledged,
and they love to circle and scream far above the
mountain's crest all the tranquil afternoon. Sometimes one sees them against the slowly changing
and swelling thunder-heads that so often burden
the horizon at this season.

It is on the dewy August mornings that one notices
the webs of the little spiders in the newly mown
meadows. They look like gossamer napkins spread
out upon the grass, — thousands of napkins far
and near. The farmer looks upon it as a sign of
rain; but the napkins are there every day; only a
heavier dew makes them more pronounced one
morning than another.

Along the paths where my walks oftenest lead me
in August, in rather low, bushy, wet grounds, the
banner flower is a species of purple boneset, or trumpet-weed, so called, I suppose, because its stem is
hollow. It often stands up seven or eight feet high,
crowned with a great mass of dull purple bloom, and
leads the ranks of lesser weeds and plants like a
great chieftain. Its humbler servitors are white
boneset and swamp milkweed, while climbing boneset trails its wreaths over the brookside bushes not
far away. A much more choice and brilliant purple,
like some invasion of metropolitan fashion into a
rural congregation, is given to a near-by marsh by the
purple loosestrife. During the latter half of August
the bog is all aflame with it. There is a wonderful

style about this plant, either singly or in masses. Its
suggestion is as distinctly feminine as that of the
trumpet-weed is masculine.

When the poet personifies August, let him fill her
arms with some of these flowers, or place upon her
brows a spray of wild clematis, which during this
month throws its bridal wreaths so freely over our
bushy, unkempt waysides and fence corners. After
you have crowned and adored your personified
August in this way, then give the finishing touch
with the scarlet raceme of the cardinal flower,
flaming from the sheaf of ranker growths in her
arms. How this brilliant bit of color, glassing
itself in a dark, still pool, lights up and affects the
vague, shadowy background upon which it is projected!

In August the "waters blossom." This is the
term the country people in my section apply to a
phenomenon which appears in the more sluggish
streams and ponds during this month. When ex-
amined closely, the water appears to be filled with
particles of very fine meal. I suspect, though I do
not know, that these floating particles are the spores
of some species of fresh-water alga; or they may
be what are called zoöspores. The algæ are at their
rankest during August. Great masses of some
species commonly called "frogs' spawn" rise to the
surface of the Hudson and float up and down with
the tide, — green unclean-looking masses, many

yards in extent. The dog-star seems to invoke these fermenting masses from the deep. They suggest decay, but they are only the riot of the lower forms of vegetable life.

August, too, is the month of the mushrooms, — those curious abnormal flowers of a hidden or subterranean vegetation, invoked by heat and moisture from darkness and decay as the summer wanes. Do they not suggest something sickly and uncanny in Nature? her unwholesome dreams and night fancies, her pale superstitions ; her myths and legends and occult lore taking shape in them, spectral and fantastic, at times hinting something libidinous and unseemly: vegetables with gills, fibreless, bloodless; earth-flesh, often offensive, unclean, immodest, often of rare beauty and delicacy, of many shades and colors — creamy white, red, yellow, brown, — now the hue of an orange, now of a tomato, now of a potato, some edible, some poisonous, some shaped like spread umbrellas, some like umbrellas reversed by the wind, — the sickly whims and fancies of Nature, some imp of the earth mocking and travestying the things of the day. Under my evergreens I saw a large white disk struggling up through the leaves and the débris like the full moon through clouds and vapors. This simile is doubtless suggested to my mind by a line of a Southern poet, Madison Cawein, which I look upon as one of the best descriptive lines in recent nature poetry : —

" The slow toadstool comes bulging, moony white,
Through loosening loam.' '

Sometimes this moon of the loam is red, or golden, or bronzed; or it is so small that it suggests only a star. The shy wood folk seem to know the edible mushrooms, and I notice often eat away the stalk and nibble at the top or pileus.

One day two friends came to see me with something wrapped up in their handkerchiefs. They said they had brought their dinner with them, — they had gathered it in the woods as they came along, —beefsteak mushrooms. The beefsteak was duly cooked and my friends ate of it with a relish. A portion was left, which my dog attacked rather doubtingly, and then turned away from, with the look of one who has been cheated. Mock-meat, that is what it was, — a curious parody upon a steak, as the dog soon found out. I know a man who boasts of having identified and eaten seventy-five different species. When the season is a good one for mushrooms, he snaps his fingers at the meat trust, even going to the extent of drying certain kinds to be used for soup in the winter.

The decay of a mushroom parodies that of real flesh, — a kind of unholy rotting ending in blackness and stench. Some species imitate jelly, — mock calves'-foot jelly, which soon melts down and becomes an uncanny mass. Occasionally I see a blue-

gilled mushroom, — an infusion of indigo in its cells.
How forbidding it looks! Yesterday in the August
woods I saw a tiny mushroom like a fairy parasol of
a Japanese type, — its top delicately fluted.

During the steaming, dripping, murky, and
muggy dog-days that sometimes come the latter
half of August, how this fungus growth runs riot in
the woods and in the fields too, — a kind of sacri-
legious vegetation mocking Nature's saner and more
wholesome handiwork, — the flowers of death,
vegetable spectres.

August days are for the most part tranquil days;
the fret and hurry of the season are over. We are on
the threshold of autumn. Nature dreams and med-
itates; her veins no longer thrill with the eager,
frenzied sap; she ripens and hardens her growths;
she concentrates; she begins to make ready for
winter. The buds for next year are formed during
this month, and her nuts and seeds and bulbs finish
storing up food for the future plant.

From my outlook upon the Hudson the days are
placid, the river is placid, the boughs of the trees
gently wag, the bees make vanishing-lines through
the air. The passing boats create a great commotion
in the water, converting it from a cool, smooth,
shadowy surface to one pulsing and agitated. The
pulsations go shoreward in long, dark, rolling, glassy
swells. The grapes are purpling in the vineyard;
the apples and pears are coloring in the orchard;

the corn is glazing in the field; the oats are ripe for the cradle; grasshoppers poise and shuffle above the dry road; yellow butterflies mount upward face to face; thistledown drifts by on the breeze; a sparrow sings fitfully now and then; dusty wheelmen go by on their summer vacation tours; boats appear upon the river loaded with gay excursionists, and on every hand the stress and urge of life have abated.

Slide Mountain, Catskills. Drawing by Jean Fader.

THE SPELL OF THE YOSEMITE

I

YOSEMITE won my heart at once, as it seems to win the hearts of all who visit it. In my case many things helped to do it, but I am sure a robin, the first I had seen since leaving home, did his part. He struck the right note, he brought the scene home to me, he supplied the link of association. There he was, running over the grass or perching on the fence, or singing from a tree-top in the old familiar way. Where the robin is at home, there at home am I. But many other things helped to win my heart to the Yosemite — the whole character of the scene, not only its beauty and sublimity, but the air of peace and protection, and of homelike seclusion that pervades it; the charm of a nook, a retreat, combined with the power and grandeur of nature in her sternest moods.

After passing from the hotel at El Portal along the foaming and roaring Merced River, and amid the tumbled confusion of enormous granite boulders shaken down from the cliffs above, you cross the threshold of the great valley as into some vast house or hall carved out of the mountains, and at once feel the spell of the brooding calm and sheltered seclusion that pervades it. You pass suddenly from the tumultuous, the chaotic, into the ordered, the tranquil, the restful, which seems enhanced by the power and grandeur that encompass them about. You can hardly be prepared for the hush that suddenly falls upon the river and for the gentle rural and sylvan character of much that surrounds you; the peace of the fields, the seclusion of the woods, the privacy of sunny glades, the enchantment of falls and lucid waters, with a touch of human occupancy here and there — all this, set in that enormous granite frame, three or four thousand feet high, ornamented with domes and spires and peaks still higher,— it is all this that wins your heart and fills your imagination in the Yosemite.

As you ride or walk along the winding road up the level valley amid the noble pines and spruces and oaks, and past the groves and bits of meadow and the camps of many tents, and the huge mossy granite boulders here and there reposing in the shade of the trees, with the full, clear, silent river winding through the plain near you, you are all the time aware of those huge vertical walls, their faces scarred and niched, streaked with color, or glistening with moisture, and animated with waterfalls, rising up on either hand, thousands of feet high, not architectural, or like something builded, but like the sides and the four corners of the globe itself. What an

impression of mass and of power and of grandeur in
repose filters into you as you walk along! El Capitan stands there showing its simple sweeping lines
through the trees as you approach, like one of the
veritable pillars of the firmament. How long we are
nearing it and passing it! It is so colossal that it
seems near while it is yet far off. It is so simple that
the eye takes in its naked grandeur at a glance. It
demands of you a new standard of size which you
cannot at once produce. It is as clean and smooth
as the flank of a horse, and as poised and calm as
a Greek statue. It curves out toward the base as if
planted there to resist the pressure of worlds —
probably the most majestic single granite column
or mountain buttress on the earth. Its summit is
over three thousand feet above you. Across the valley, nearly opposite, rise the Cathedral Rocks to
nearly the same height, while farther along, beyond
El Capitan, the Three Brothers shoulder the sky at
about the same dizzy height. Near the head of the
great valley, North Dome, perfect in outline as if
turned in a lathe, and its brother, the Half Dome
(or shall we say half-brother?) across the valley,
look down upon Mirror Lake from an altitude of
over four thousand feet. These domes suggest enormous granite bubbles if such were possible pushed
up from below and retaining their forms through
the vast geologic ages. Of course they must have
weathered enormously, but as the rock seems to

peel off in concentric sheets, their forms are preserved.

II

One warm, bright Sunday near the end of April, six of us walked up from the hotel to Vernal and Nevada Falls, or as near to them as we could get, and took our fill of the tumult of foaming waters struggling with the wreck of huge granite cliffs: so impassive and immobile the rocks, so impetuous and reckless and determined the onset of the waters, till the falls are reached, when the obstructed river seems to find the escape and the freedom it was so eagerly seeking. Better to be completely changed into foam and spray by one single leap of six hundred feet into empty space, the river seems to say, than be forever baffled and tortured and torn on this rack of merciless boulders.

We followed the zigzagging trail up the steep side of the valley, touching melting snow-banks in its upper courses, passing huge granite rocks also melting in the slow heat of the geologic ages, pausing to take in the rugged, shaggy spruces and pines that sentineled the mountain-sides here and there, or resting our eyes upon Liberty Cap, which carries its suggestive form a thousand feet or more above the Nevada Fall. What beauty, what grandeur attended us that day! the wild tumult of waters, the snow-white falls, the motionless avalanches of granite rocks, and the naked granite shaft, Liberty Cap, dominating all!

And that night, too, when we sat around a big camp-fire near our tents in the valley, and saw the full moon come up and look down upon us from behind Sentinel Rock, and heard the intermittent booming of Yosemite Falls sifting through the spruce trees that towered around us, and felt the tender, brooding spirit of the great valley, itself touched to lyric intensity by the grandeurs on every hand, steal in upon us, and possess our souls—surely that was a night none of us can ever forget. As Yosemite can stand the broad, searching light of midday and not be cheapened, so its enchantments can stand the light of the moon and the stars and not be rendered too vague and impalpable.

III

Going from the Grand Cañon to Yosemite is going from one sublimity to another of a different order. The cañon is the more strange, unearthly, apocryphal, appeals more to the imagination, and is the more overwhelming in its size, its wealth of color, and its multitude of suggestive forms. But for quiet majesty and beauty, with a touch of the sylvan and pastoral, too, Yosemite stands alone. One could live with Yosemite, camp in it, tramp in it, winter and summer in it, and find nature in her tender and human, almost domestic moods, as well as in her grand and austere. But I do not think one could ever feel at home in or near the Grand Cañon; it is too unlike anything we have ever known upon the earth; it is like a vision of some strange colossal city uncovered from the depth of geologic time. You may have come to it, as we did, from the Petrified Forests, where you saw the silicified trunks of thousands of gigantic trees or tree ferns, that grew millions of years ago, most of them uncovered, but many of them protruding from banks of clay and gravel, and in their interiors rich in all the colors of the rainbow, and you wonder if you may not now be gazing upon some petrified antediluvian city of temples and holy places exhumed by mysterious hands and opened up to the vulgar gaze of to-day. You look into it from above and from another world and you descend into it at your peril. Yosemite you enter as into a gigantic hall and make your own; the cañon you gaze down upon, and are an alien, whether you enter it or not. Yosemite is carved out of the most majestic and enduring of all rocks, granite; the Grand Cañon is carved out of one of the most beautiful, but perishable, red Carboniferous sandstone and limestone. There is a maze of beautiful and intricate lines in the latter, a wilderness of temple-like forms and monumental remains, and noble architectural profiles that delight while they bewilder the eye. Yosemite has much greater simplicity, and is much nearer the classic standard of beauty. Its grand and austere features predominate, of course, but underneath these and adorning them are many touches of the idyllic and the picturesque. Its many waterfalls fluttering like white lace against its vertical granite walls, its smooth, level floor, its noble pines and oaks, its open glades, its sheltering groves, its bright, clear, winding river, its soft voice of many waters, its flowers, its birds, its grass, its verdure, even its orchards of blooming apple trees, all inclosed in this tremendous granite frame — what an unforgettable picture it all makes, what a blending of the sublime and the homelike and familiar it all is! It is the waterfalls that make the granite alive, and bursting into bloom as it were. What a touch they give! how they enliven the scene! What music they evoke from these harps of stone!

The first leap of Yosemite Falls is sixteen hundred feet — sixteen hundred feet of a compact mass of snowy rockets shooting downward and bursting into spray around which rainbows flit and hover. The next leap is four hundred feet, and the last six hundred. We tried to get near the foot and inspect the hidden recess in which this airy spirit again took on a more tangible form of still, running water, but the spray over a large area fell like a summer shower, drenching the trees and the rocks, and holding the inquisitive tourist off at a safe distance. We had to beat a retreat with dripping garments before we had got within fifty yards of the foot of the fall. At first I was surprised at the volume of water that came hurrying out of the hidden recess of dripping rocks and trees — a swiftly flowing stream, thirty or forty feet wide, and four or five feet deep. How could that comparatively narrow curtain of white spray up there give birth to such a full robust stream? But I saw that in making the tremendous leap from the top of the precipice, the stream was suddenly drawn out, as we stretch a rubber band in our hands, and that the solid and massive current below was like the rubber again relaxed. The strain was over, and the united waters deepened and slowed up over their rocky bed.

Yosemite for a home or a camp, the Grand Cañon for a spectacle. I have spoken of the robin I saw in Yosemite Valley. Think how forlorn and out of place a robin would seem in the Grand Cañon! What would he do there? There is no turf for him to inspect, and there are no trees for him to perch on. I should as soon expect to find him amid the pyramids of Egypt, or amid the ruins of Karnak. The bluebird was in the Yosemite also, and the water-ouzel haunted the lucid waters.

I noticed a peculiarity of the oak in Yosemite that I never saw elsewhere[1] — a fluid or outflowing condition of the growth aboveground, such as one usually sees in the roots of trees — so that it tended to en-

[1] I have since observed the same trait in the oaks in Georgia —probably a characteristic of this tree in southern latitudes.

velop and swallow, as it were, any solid object with which it came in contact. If its trunk touched a point of rock, it would put out great oaken lips several inches in extent as if to draw the rock into its maw. If a dry limb was cut or broken off, a foot from the trunk, these thin oaken lips would slowly creep out and envelop it — a sort of Western omnivorous trait appearing in the trees.

Whitman refers to "the slumbering and liquid trees." These Yosemite oaks recall his expression more surely than any of our Eastern trees.

The reader may create for himself a good image of Yosemite by thinking of a section of seven or eight miles of the Hudson River, midway of its course, as emptied of its water and deepened three thousand feet or more, having the sides nearly vertical, with snow-white waterfalls fluttering against them here and there, the famous spires and domes planted along the rim, and the landscape of groves and glades, with its still, clear winding river, occupying the bottom.

IV

One cannot look upon Yosemite or walk beneath its towering walls without the question arising in his mind, How did all this happen? What were the agents that brought it about? There has been a great geologic drama enacted here; who or what were the star actors? There are two other valleys in this part of the Sierra, Hetch-Hetchy and King's River, that are almost identical in their main features, though the Merced Yosemite is the widest of the three. Each of them is a tremendous chasm in the granite rock, with nearly vertical walls, domes, El Capitans, and Sentinel and Cathedral Rocks, and waterfalls — all modeled on the same general plan. I believe there is nothing just like this trio of Yosemites anywhere else on the globe.

Guided by one's ordinary sense or judgment alone, one's judgment as developed and disciplined by the everyday affairs of life and the everyday course of nature, one would say on beholding Yosemite that here is the work of exceptional and extraordinary agents or world-building forces. It is as surprising and exceptional as would be a cathedral in a village street, or a gigantic sequoia in a grove of our balsam firs. The approach to it up the Merced River does not prepare one for any such astonishing spectacle as awaits one. The rushing, foaming water amid the tumbled confusion of huge granite rocks and the open V-shaped valley, are nothing very remarkable or unusual. Then suddenly you are on the threshold of this hall of the elder gods. Demons and furies might lurk in the valley below, but here is the abode of the serene, beneficent Olympian deities. All is so calm, so hushed, so friendly, yet so towering, so stupendous, so unspeakably beautiful. You are in a mansion carved out of the granite foundations of the earth, with walls two or three thousand feet high, hung here and there with snow-white waterfalls, and supporting the blue sky on domes and pinnacles still higher. Oh, the calmness and majesty of the scene! the evidence of such tremendous activity of some force, some agent, and now so tranquil, so sheltering, so beneficent!

That there should be two or three Yosemites in the Sierra not very far apart, all with the main features singularly alike, is very significant — as if this kind of valley was latent in the granite of that region — some peculiarity of rock structure that lends itself readily to these formations. The Sierra lies beyond the southern limit of the great continental ice-sheet of late Tertiary times, but it nursed and reared many local glaciers, and to the eroding power of these its Yosemites are partly due. But water was at work here long before the ice — eating down into the granite and laying open the mountain for the ice to begin its work. Ice may come, and ice may go, says the river, but I go on forever. Water tends to make a V-shaped valley, ice a U-shaped one, though in the Hawaiian Islands, where water erosion alone has taken place, the prevailing form of the valleys is that of the U-shaped. Yosemite approximates to this shape, and ice has certainly played a part in its formation. But the glacier seems to have stopped at the outlet of the great valley; it did not travel beyond the gigantic hall it had helped to excavate. The valley of the Merced from the mouth of Yosemite downward is an open valley strewn with huge angular granite rocks and shows no signs of glaciation whatever. The reason of this abruptness is quite beyond my ken. It is to me a plausible theory that when the granite that forms the Sierra was lifted or squeezed up by the shrinking of the earth, large fissures and crevasses may have occurred, and that Yosemite and kindred valleys may be the result of the action of water and ice in enlarging these original chasms. Little wonder that the earlier geologists, such as Whitney, were led to attribute the exceptional character of these valleys to exceptional and extraordinary agents — to sudden faulting or dislocation of the earth's crust. But geologists are becoming more and more loath to call in the cataclysmal to explain any feature of the topography of the land. Not to the thunder or the lightning, to earthquake or volcano, to the forces of upheaval or dislocation, but to the still, small voice of the rain and the winds, of the frost and the snow, — the gentle forces now and here active all about us, carving the valleys and reducing the mountains, and changing the courses of rivers, — to these, as Lyell taught us, we are to look in nine cases out of ten, yes, in ninety-nine out of a hundred, to account for the configuration of the continents.

The geologists of our day, while not agreeing as to the amount of work done respectively by ice and water, yet agree that to the latter the larger proportion of the excavation is to be ascribed. At any rate between them both they have turned out one of the most beautiful and stupendous pieces of mountain carving to be found upon the earth.